Under the Sun

A Search for Meaning

Under the Sun

A Search for Meaning

Wes Feltner, Ph.D.

Critical Mass Books
Davenport, Florida
www.criticalmasspublishing.com

Cover Design   Eowyn Riggins
Interior Layout   Rachel Greene

ISBN: 978-1-947153-24-0

Chapter One

"The Search for Meaning"

All of us have dark thoughts. Things we don't dare say out loud. Thoughts better kept inside. Then, every once in a while, someone comes along who has the courage to actually say what we wanted to say. Such moments are usually not very comfortable. It is not always received well. It is usually met with a sense of shock or even outrage. People dismiss it. Ignore it. Explain it away. Or aren't sure how to respond. That's exactly what happened to one of the most famous authors of the 20th century. Among his published works were great books such as *Mere Christianity*, *The Screwtape Letters*, and his most popular books (on which a movie series was based)–*The Chronicles of Narnia*.

His name was Clive, but most people know him as C.S. Lewis.

C.S. Lewis died more than 55 years ago—on the very same day that President Kennedy was assassinated— and he remains a beloved figure today, particularly in Christian circles. Lewis was known for his literary creativity, robust theology, and intellectual dexterity. To those outside the Christian faith, Lewis was highly respected. To those within the Christian faith, he was one of the most known, celebrated, and frequently quoted authors of his time.

But there is one book by Lewis that is not all that widely celebrated, largely because most people don't know exactly what to do with it. For in it, Lewis has the courage to say things that most people are afraid to say out loud. It's called, *A Grief Observed*. In it, Lewis writes:

> *Where is God? When you are happy, so happy you have no sense of needing Him...you will be, so it feels, welcomed with open arms. But go to Him when your need is desperate, when all other help is vain and what do you find? A door slammed in your face, a sound of bolting and double bolting on the inside. After that, silence. You may as well turn away. The longer you wait, the more emphatic the silence becomes. There are no lights in the windows. It might be an empty house. Was it ever inhabited? Not that I am in danger of ceasing to believe in God. The real danger is of coming to believe such dreadful things about Him. The conclusion I dread is not 'There is no God' but 'This is what God is really like'....It doesn't matter whether you grip the arms of the dentist's chair or let your hands lie in your lap. The drill drills on.*

C.S. Lewis said that? THE C.S. Lewis? Yes, Lewis wrote those words...shortly after his wife died of cancer. She was only 45-years-old. In his grief, suffering, and confusion, Lewis was willing to say out loud what most people of the Christian faith keep suppressed inside.

You see, even the great C.S. Lewis found himself in a situation he could not understand. He was not able to find meaning in a situation that seemed meaningless. The truth is, like Lewis, we all find ourselves, from time-to-time, searching for meaning in a fallen world. We have questions and life doesn't seem to have answers. And neither does God, so it seems.

Much like Lewis's *A Grief Observed,* the Bible also includes a book most Christians don't know what to do with. They don't know how to handle its raw honesty and willingness to say out loud what most don't have to courage to say. That book is the book of *Ecclesiastes.* It is not like Proverbs, full of pithy guidelines for life. It's not like the Psalms, full of worship and praise with the occasional lament of desperation. And it is certainly not like the Song of Solomon, full of things like...well, maybe you should read that one for yourself! Ecclesiastes? It is full of questions that seem to have no answers, a God who it appears to have left you to enjoy what you can while you can in the seemingly vain life He has given you. It is uncomfortable, raw with honesty, and it forces you to take a hard look at life, whether you want to or not.

What we find instead is an honest reality check about life. The book forces us to admit something is wrong. The book of Ecclesiastes is to the Bible what Johnny Cash was to country music. Cash was known as the "Man in Black." And the reason he always wore back was "*for the poor and the beaten down, livin' in the hopeless, hungry side of town.*" Cash knew there was something wrong with the world. That things were not as they should be. And his wearing black was a constant reminder that "while he would love to wear a rainbow everyday" that was not the reality of the world in which we live. The book of Ecclesiastes does the exact same thing.

We would love for every day to be filled with butterflies and kittens and the knowledge that everything is going to be fine. But the reality is that there *is* darkness in the world. Life doesn't always make sense. There are often far more questions than answers. And sometimes, if we are honest like Lewis, it appears God doesn't give a rip.

In the movie, *Grand Canyon*, there is a scene in which an attorney's car breaks down on the side of the road and he has to call for a tow truck. Before the tow truck gets there, the lawyer is harassed by gang members. The tow truck driver—played by Danny Glover— pulls up and says, "*The world ain't supposed to be like this. Maybe you don't know that, but this ain't the way it's supposed to be. I'm supposed to be able to do my job without asking you if I can. And he's supposed to be able to wait with this car without you ripping him off. Everything is supposed to be different than what it is.*"

Does that resonate with you? Do you ever look at the world and think, "*This just doesn't make sense?*"

I have written this book to stimulate an honest conversation about life in this world and how we can find meaning in it. I want to encourage people, and particularly Christians, to not be afraid of entering into the darkness and asking the hard questions. To get their head out of the proverbial sands and enter into the brokenness. To have the guts, and even the faith, to admit the world is not sugar and spice and everything nice. But to do so will be challenging. It will mean entering into issues and questions that will make you uncomfortable. It will mean a willingness to be pushed to the edge, but with good purpose. So, as you read through these pages, make the decision to do your soul good by committing yourself to learn and comprehend what God has for you. You may learn things you didn't know were in the Bible and in doing so will begin to experience a freedom to say things you didn't know you could have the freedom to say.

But before we dive into to some of the hard and challenging questions we are forced to face in the book of Ecclesiastes, we must first understand how the book of Ecclesiastes is structured. While this may seem insignificant at first, it will prove to be very important later on.

Let's begin with the author of the book. In the opening sentence we read, *"The words of the preacher, the son of David, King in Jerusalem."* On the surface, this would appear to be Solomon. This is the most commonly accepted view. King of Jerusalem: Check. Son of David: Check. Filled with wisdom (1:16): Check. Has enormous wealth and possessions (chapter 2): Check. So, on the surface, it appears that the author is Solomon.

But I believe a closer look will prove that the author is someone *playing the character* of Solomon (or a Solomon-like figure) in a form of ancient theater. (And by the way, even if you don't find my arguments convincing, it won't change the message of the book). But this view is the foundation from which we will be looking at the entire book of Ecclesiastes.

So why do I believe we need to embrace a different view of authorship than the majority held Solomon view? First, let's take another look at the beginning of the book, *"The words of the preacher, the son of David, King in Jerusalem."* The reader should note right away that Solomon is not mentioned by name. Now you might think this is insignificant. Many biblical authors wrote books without putting themselves in the introduction. True, but in the other books that are clearly written by Solomon, this pattern is always followed. For example, in the beginning of Proverbs Solomon is specifically mentioned by name as author. The same is true with the Song of Solomon. So, Ecclesiastes bucks the trend. Why would he be mentioned by name as the author of one book, but not another? Clearly this not enough to make any solid conclusions, but it is something worth our attention. Let's look further.

Second, the word *son* in the phrase *"the son of David"* is actually the generic Hebrew word for *descendant*. It is not specifying a direct son. It simply means someone from David's line. Of course, this could be Solomon, but it doesn't have to be.

Third, in Ecclesiastes 1:12, it says, *"I, the preacher have been king over Israel."* This Hebrew sentence is in the past tense. That's a problem if this is Solomon because Solomon died as king. There was not a point in his life when he would have been able to look back at a time when he "was king".

Fourth, in Ecclesiastes 1:16, we read, *"I said in my heart, 'I have acquired great wisdom, surpassing <u>all who were over Jerusalem before me.</u>'"*

Then in Ecclesiastes 2:9, it says, "*So I became great and surpassed all who were before me in Jerusalem.*" This doesn't seem to fit either. Before Solomon there were not many kings. Only David and Saul. Why would you use the expression "all who were before me" if the "all" was only two?

And probably most convincing of all (at least for me) is the fact that there are clearly two voices in the book. For example, in 1:1 we read, "*The words of the preacher.*" But later on in the same chapter (1:12) we read, "*I, the preacher.*" There is a change of voice, a change of speakers. And the same thing also happens at the end of the book. Ecclesiastes 12:9 says, "*Besides being wise, the preacher also taught the people knowledge, weighing and studying and arranging many proverbs with great care.*" Based on these reasons, I believe we are not dealing with a book written by Solomon, but a different kind of Ancient Near Eastern literature that is still given to us by the inspiration of God.

Chapter Two

"Live Like You Were Dying"

So, what is the structure for Ecclesiastes? Due to the fact that there is one voice in the beginning speaking of *the preacher, and another* voice that picks up soon after, and continues through the rest of the book, the book of Ecclesiastes is likely a form of wisdom literature, common in the ancient near East, known as fictional autobiography. In the ancient near East, it was extremely common for a sage or wise man to teach wisdom in the form of a story. Think Aesop's fables. In this form of literature, one would take on the persona of a famous person (even a king-type figure) in order to teach someone about the wisdom of life.

In the case of Ecclesiastes, it is a father teaching his son about the searching for meaning in life. He does this by assuming a famous persona that people would know, someone easily recognized as an expert. The narrator teaches about the meaning of life through Solomon, or Solomon-like figure, because if anyone could have found meaning of life it would have been someone of that kind of stature.

To give an example, my son loves football. He loves to watch football, play football, and talk football. He is obsessed with football. So, what if I wanted to teach my son about wisdom in life or how to find meaning in the world, but instead of just teaching him random principles, I told him a story. The story of someone like Tom Brady. Someone who has it all, who has reached the pinnacle of success in sports. Surely, if meaning, happiness, and understanding in life could be found, someone like Tom Brady would find it.

Make sense?

Evangelical commentator Tremper Longman says, "So why does Ecclesiastes give the impression that it is written by Solomon? Because in ancient times it was very common for people to write fictional autobiographies. That is, in order to communicate his message, a writer would take on a persona of someone famous, like Solomon. This was not done in order to deceive anybody. In fact, most of these were based on the life of someone from history. Many evangelicals think Ecclesiastes is the same kind of book. The author has taken a well-known figure from history and used that person's life to make a spiritual point."

I am convinced this is what makes the most sense given the structure of Ecclesiastes.

So, who is this voice? Who is *the preacher* mentioned in Ecclesiastes 1:1. The Hebrew word for the preacher is Qoheleth (pronounced CO-HELL-ITH). This is more than simply a Hebrew word, it is a Hebrew name. So why do the translators translate it as "the preacher?" Because the meaning of the name is "one who assembles" like a preacher. But the word is not a position, it is a person.

So the main character of the book is a person named Qoheleth. He is the Solomon-like king the father (narrator) uses to teach his son about meaning in the world. [Which is why, by the way, there are so many parallels to Solomon in the book].

Qoheleth's main point, as you will see again and again, is that life is full of vanity. *"Vanity of vanities, all is vanity."* This simply means that everything is meaningless. All is empty.

Like being a Chicago Bears fan.

Now, before you label him a Debbie Downer, someone who is overly pessimistic or depressing, you need to realize that he comes to this conclusion with rational reasons. Don't forget this is WISDOM literature. Qoheleth has reasons for his conclusion. He was not just having a bad hair day. Or upset because his team lost the game. He has been on a life-long search to find meaning in the world and has come up empty. He will tell you his journey, inform you of his process, and give you convincing reasons why you should come to the same conclusion that he has.

But of all the reasons he will give you, there is one primary reason above all others. Death! (You promised you would not check out even if the journey gets challenging).

"But all this I laid to heart, examining it all, how the righteous and the wise and their deeds are in the hand of God. Whether it is love or hate, man does not know; both are before him. It is the same for all, since the same event happens to the righteous and the wicked, to the good and the evil, to the clean and the unclean, to him who sacrifices and him who does not sacrifice. As the good one is, so is the sinner, and he who swears is as he who shuns an oath. This is an evil in all that is done under the sun, that the same event happens to all." (Ecc 9:1)

"It is better to go to the house of mourning than to go to the house of feasting, for this is the end of all mankind...." (Ecc 7:2)

According to Qoheleth, life is meaningless because it is temporary. He is not saying life is not fun, or enjoyable, or full of great memories, he is simply saying that those things cannot give you meaning because they are all temporary. And it is death that makes them that way. Like C.S. Lewis, he had the courage to say aloud what he really thought about the emptiness of life. What many of us think, but haven't the courage to admit out loud.

Because of death, life is meaningless.

Now you may not like his conclusion but you cannot argue with his reasoning. Can you make a lot of money and enjoy it? Yes. Get married, have kids, and live a good life? Totally. Experience success and accomplishments in life that will make you proud of all your hard work? Most definitely. But, none of those things will last. And why will they not last? Death. Death is the only certain thing in life, and that makes everything we accomplish in this life temporary vapor and, therefore, empty and meaningless. Don't you see, the temporary nature of life is what makes life impossible to provide meaning.

Of course, the pessimist inside you might respond, "Well then why should we care about anything? Why should we even live if that is the conclusion?" Qoheleth has an answer for you:

> *"Behold, what I have seen to be good and fitting is to eat and drink and find enjoyment in all the toil with which one toils under the sun the few days of his life that God has given him, for this is his lot. Everyone also to whom God has given wealth and possessions and power to enjoy them, and to accept his lot and rejoice in his toil--this is the gift of God." (Ecc 5:18)*

If you prefer the modern-day expression of this, think Dave Matthews band as he sings "Eat, Drink and Be Merry for tomorrow you'll die." If death is inevitable, then the best thing we can do is to enjoy what we can while we can. Like when Andy, in Shawshank Redemption, tells Red, "Either get busy living or get busy dying."

Go to Starbucks and get a latte. Eat that piece of chocolate cake. Read your favorite book and sunbath at the beach. Hug those grandchildren. Enjoy your manicured lawn. Laugh at your favorite comedy. Or as Tim McGraw sings about, "go skydiving and Rocky Mountain climbing. Live like you were dying."

That's because if there is one thing that is true in life...we are.

Chapter Three

"Caution and Balance"

In the Woody Allen movie, *Annie Hall*, there is a young boy named Alvy Singer. Alvy refuses to do his homework because he just learned the universe is expanding. The world is going to end. So, Alvy rightly surmises that if the world is going to end why should he have to do his homework? (I wish I had thought of this in school). Alvy's mom, who is quite concerned for her son, takes him to see a doctor.

The following is the conversation between *Mom*, **Alvy**, and the doctor:

> Mom: "He's been depressed and all of a sudden he can't do anything."
>
> Doctor: "Why are you depressed, Alvy?"
>
> Mom: "Tell Dr. Flicker. It's something he read."

Doctor: "Something you read, huh?"

Alvy: "The universe is expanding."

Doctor: "The universe is expanding?"

Alvy: "Well, the universe is everything, and if it's expanding, someday it will break apart and that will be the end of everything."

Mom: "Why is that your business? He's not doing his homework."

Alvy: "What's the point?"

Mom: "What's the universe got to do with it? You're here in Brooklyn. Brooklyn is not expanding."

Doctor: "It won't be expanding for billions of years yet, Alvy. And we've got to try to enjoy ourselves while we're here."

Little Alvy is the grown up Qoheleth. Do you see Alvy's argument, "If the universe is expanding, if it's all going to end, what's the point?" That is the argument Qoheleth makes in Ecclesiastes. In fact, it is this perspective that has caused some scholars to believe that Ecclesiastes is describing life without God. This idea, of course, is nonsense. Not only does Qoheleth frequently mention God, but everyone in the ancient near East believed in God. "The fool says in his heart 'There is no God'".

Oh no, Qoheleth has not come to this conclusion because there is no God, he has come to this conclusion BECAUSE of God. This is the hand God has dealt us. This is the lot we've been given (as Qoheleth sees it).

It is similar to C.S. Lewis. If you take an honest look at life, sometimes it will appear God doesn't care at all. Doors shut, double bolted, followed by silence. Qoheleth believes in God, and he believes this is how God set it up.

And still…it is all vanity.

So, what do we do with that kind of honesty? Many Christians take the "quick fix" approach to issues like this. They will quickly pull out Romans 8:28 when life doesn't make sense. *"All things work together for good."* That's a great verse. It is a true promise. But it doesn't solve the problem and may prove as a mere biblical Band-Aid for your broken soul.

Other will look for a quick escape. They put on their red ruby slippers and tell themselves, *"There's no place like home. There's no place like home."* Until the pain disappears or they turn so numb it doesn't really matter anymore. Pretend it is not there, a sort of personal, spiritual, and relational hibernation.

Others are quick to conform. "Never question God" they say. "Good Christians" (whatever the heck those are) don't ask questions like this. Do your duty. Serve God. Keep following the rules. This was the approach I heard in the church tradition I grew up in. Conform, and don't allow yourself to think.

The problem with each of these approaches is that they do not work and they are not good for your soul. Other than that, they are great approaches to the inconsistencies of life!

This is why I am thankful that God, in His providence, gave us Ecclesiastes. It won't let you escape the questions of life. It forces you to think. How should we approach these things?

First, **be cautious**. People can make the book of Ecclesiastes say just about anything. It is the most misquoted book in the entire Bible. It is wisdom literature, and it is very easy for someone who does not know the foundation of the book to take it out of context. It is easy to pluck a verse out and quote it to support any opinion one may have. That is why we must look at the verses in their complete context.

As an example, Ecclesiastes says, *"Bread is made for laughter, wine gladdens life, and money answers everything."* If you pull that verse out of context, you could build a whole theology on that, which would not end well. So, don't pick and choose (which only ends up misquoting) the book in order to make it say what we want it to say.

Second, **be balanced**. There are people who love all things dark. They use Ecclesiastes as an excuse to wallow in gloom. At the other end of the spectrum, some people bury their heads in the sand and act as if everything is fine, even though the world around them makes no sense. Both perspectives are wrong. There must be balance in our understanding of Ecclesiastes. I call this balance Christian *realism*. We will face the reality of life in a fallen world with the hope of Jesus Christ.

Third, we must **be honest**. We must open our minds and hearts to honestly listen and search for what God is saying. The gospel will not be good news until we have worked through it honestly.

Qoheleth and C.S. Lewis both came to the conclusion that this world does not make sense. Both Lewis and Qoheleth came to this conclusion in the face of death. Lewis had experienced the death of his wife. Qoheleth noted the end of all mankind, whether or not they were righteous. They presented their honest opinions on the meaning of life, and they were shunned for it.

But the truth is, they are in good company. I know a Man who did the same thing. A Man who never sinned, yet was treated as though he had committed every sin. I know a Man who came to give light but the world rejected him because they preferred darkness. I know a Man who loved, but whose love was rejected. I know a Man who came to give life, but, like Lewis and Qoheleth, he ended up facing death. That Man is Jesus Christ.

While Jesus was hanging on the cross, he had the courage to ask what many others have only had the courage to think: *"My God, my God, why have you forsaken me?"* This is similar to Lewis' words: *"Go to him when your need is desperate, when all other help is in vain. And what do you find? A door slammed in your face. A sound of bolting and double bolting on the inside. And after that, silence."*

Jesus faced the reality of life in a fallen world far more than Lewis or Qoheleth or anyone else ever did. But He did not run away from that reality. He faced it. And the Father was not offended by his question. That is why the gospel is good news for anyone searching for the meaning of life.

No matter how meaningless life seems at times, life is worth the living because Jesus lives.

Chapter Four

"Stuck in an Endless Cycle"

A few years ago, I came across a course offered by the University of Wyoming. It was called *Interstellar Message Composition*. It was an actual course designed to teach students how to communicate with...you guessed it—*aliens*. You may ask, "Are you sure it wasn't a class on how to parent teenagers?" No. It was a real class on communication with extraterrestrial beings. For one of the assignments, the professor asked the students to describe human beings in ten words or less.

One student wrote, "We are an adolescent species, searching for our identity."

Hmmm. There is some truth to that student's words, at least in the fact that we are all search for answers. We are all trying to find an identity, a way of making sense out of a life that often doesn't make sense.

Now that you have been introduced to the book of Ecclesiastes, the author, the structure, and overall themes, it is now time to take a deeper dive into the specific reasons why Qoheleth comes to the conclusion that all is vanity. Let's begin in chapter 1:

Vanity of vanities, all is vanity. What does a man gain by all the toil at which he toils under the sun? A generation goes, a generation comes, but the earth remains forever. The sun rises and the sun goes down. It hastens to the place where it rises. The wind blows to the south and goes around to the north, around and around goes the wind, and on its circuits, the wind returns. All the streams run into the sea, but the sea is not full to the place where the streams flow, there they flow again. All things are full of weariness and man cannot utter it. The eye is not satisfied with seeing, nor the ear filled with hearing. What has been is what will be, what has been done is what will be done. There is nothing new under the sun. Is there a thing of which it is said, "This is new?" It has already in the ages before us. There is no remembrance of former things, nor will there be any remembrance of later things yet to be among those who come after.

I have always been a fan of Bill Murray movies (most of them anyway). And one of my favorites is the movie, *Groundhog Day*. If you haven't seen it, crawl out from underneath the rock you've been living under and go watch it! That's because not only is it a classic comedy, but it will also help you understand the book of Ecclesiastes.

In the movie, Murray plays a weather man named Phil Connors who has been assigned to Punxsutawney, Pennsylvania for the annual February 2nd Groundhog Day activities. While he is there for this assignment, Phil, along with his entire crew, end up trapped in a snow storm. While stuck there, he starts reliving the *same day* over and over again, until he eventually realizes he is stuck—in Groundhog Day. Every morning he wakes up to the same music, around every corner he has the same conversation, and nothing he does (even driving his car over a cliff) can break the cycle he is stuck in.

As he comes to grips with this reality, he starts to see life differently. His attitude changes drastically. At one point in the movie he asks, "What would you do if you were stuck in one place and every day was exactly and same, and nothing you did mattered?" It is because of this feeling stuck, that nothing he does seems to matter, which leads him to say:

> *This is pitiful. A thousand people freezing their butts off, waiting to worship a rat. What a hype. Probably used to mean something in this town. They used to pull a hog out and they used to eat it. You're hypocrites. All of you. You got a problem with what I'm saying, Larry? Untie your tongue and you come out here and talk. Huh? Am I upsetting you, princess? You want a prediction about the weather? You're asking the wrong Phil. I'll give you a winter prediction. It's going to be cold, it's going to be gray, and it's going to last you for the rest of your life.*

How's that for a weather forecast?

But honestly, put yourself in Phil's situation. Imagine if you were stuck in the same situation every day. Would you feel a similar way? Have you ever felt that way? Maybe you have never been stuck in the same day, but to some degree we have all been stuck in the routine of life. Some of us do the same job every day. Maybe you drive the same commute. Maybe you sit at the same desk every day. For many of us it is sometimes a struggle to get up in the morning, especially when it feels like nothing will change.

We mow the grass, and it grows back.

We wash the dishes, and they get dirty again.

We clean the house, and the kids mess it up again.

We do the same chores over and over.

It is the same thing over and over again.

Some of us live in the same town where we were born. Some of us have never left our home state. Some of us have been married to the same person for 20, 30, or even 50 years. The spark has been replaced with routine, a marriage based on just going through the motions. We laugh at *Groundhog Day*, but for many of us this is the reality of life.

You see, while Ground Hog Day may be a comedy, it is actually a metaphor for reality. That is exactly what Qoheleth discovers about life.

Chapter Five

"Stuck on the Treadmill of Life"

What does a man gain by all the toil at which he toils under the sun?" That is the question Qoheleth is trying to answer. On one hand, there is a lot to gain in life, right? We gain memories. We gain friendships. We gain family. We gain money. We gain things. But do we? Qoheleth would say we *get* those things, but we don't actually *gain* them!

Let me illustrate.

Have you ever invested in the stock market? If you have ever talked to a financial advisor, they will tell you: if your stock goes up you did not actually gain anything. In the same way, if your stock goes down, you did not actually lose anything. That's because you haven't sold anything yet. You see, gains and loses don't actually happen until the point of sell. If you sell while the stock is up…then you gained. If you sell while the stock is down…then you lost. But gains and losses are only real at the point of sell.

The same is true, Qoheleth would argue, with life. Life is like the stock market. The problem for all of us, however, is the closing bell is death. At that point, everything is back to zero. Those memories you thought you gained… are gone. That money you thought you gained…it goes away. Again, that's not to say these things are bad, they are just temporary. That may sound depressing, but it is a very rational and logical perspective. After all, doesn't the Bible teach us that we don't take anything with us when we die?

To make matters worse, Qoheleth would say that not only do you not gain anything when life is over, but during life you are stuck on a treadmill. Like in the movie, *Groundhog Day*.

As we all know, running on a treadmill doesn't actually get us anywhere. We turn it on. We walk or run. We sweat. We burn calories. It feels like progress. But when we are finished, we are right where we started.

That is the endless cycle of life. As Qoheleth says, "*A generation goes and a generation comes.*" Life is like shark teeth. When one falls out another one grows back. As generations get older, they see themselves being replaced, with younger people filling their roles. The wrinkles on our faces and the pictures on our walls may say that we have traveled many miles. It will feel like we've done a lot. But, in reality, we have simply been on the treadmill of humanity.

"The sun rises and the sun goes down, and it hastens to the place where it rises." Think about the sun. It comes up in the morning, it shines all day long, then it finally sets. It comes up again. It shines all day long until it sets. It repeats this cycle over and over again. Like a treadmill. *"The wind blows to the south and goes around to the north, around and around goes the wind, and on its circuits, the wind returns."* Think about the wind. It blows and it blows. We never hear a weatherman say, "The forecast next week is that we are going to run out of wind."

Wind keeps going in its cycle.

"All the streams run to the sea, but the sea is not full to the place where the streams flow, theory they flow again." Think about water. It evaporates from the ocean, goes over the mountain, rains, comes down into the rivers, and then goes back to the ocean. The cycle repeats over and over. Another treadmill. You might argue that there is change because the season's change, from summer, to fall, to winter, and to spring. Even *they* represent a cycle.

"What has been is what will be, and what has been done is what will be done, and there is nothing new under the sun." Think of it this way. You are born in a hospital. You have no teeth. You have to wear diapers. Someone cares for you around the clock. At the end of life what happens? You lose your teeth, you have to wear diapers, and someone cares for you around the clock until you finally die in, probably, a *hospital*. In between those two major life events, you pay bills, and more bills come.

Whether we like it or not this is the treadmill of life.

Chapter Six

"Lather-Rinse-Repeat"

"Value this time in your life, kids. This is the time in your life when you have choices. It goes by so fast. When you are a teenager, you think that you can do anything, and you do. Your twenties are a blur. In your thirties you make a little money, raise a family, and wonder, 'What happened to my twenties?' In your forties, you grow a pot belly and another chin. The music starts to get too loud and one of your old girlfriends becomes a grandmother. In your fifties, you have a minor surgery – you call it a 'procedure.' In your sixties, you have a major surgery and the music is still loud but that doesn't matter because you can no longer hear it. In your seventies, you and the wife move to Florida and you start having dinner at 2 in the afternoon, lunch at 10 in the morning,

and breakfast the night before. You spend most of your time wandering around malls looking for the ultimate low-fat yogurt and muttering, 'How come the kids don't call?' In your eighties you have a major stroke and end up babbling to a Jamaican nurse whom your wife can't stand, but who you end up calling, 'Momma.'"

T hose are the words of Billy Crystal's character in the movie *City Slickers*, as he addresses a class of confused 4th graders! It's funny because it's true. It is the same point Qoheleth is making. If we took an honest look at humanity, creation, and life itself, we would come to the conclusion that everything and everyone is stuck in an endless cycle. The things we read in Dr. Seuss books are not true.

"Oh the places that you will go. You'll be on your way up. You'll be seeing great sites. You'll join the high flyers who soar to high Heights. You won't lag behind, because you'll have the speed. You'll pass the whole gang and you will soon take the lead. Wherever you fly, you'll be the best of the best and wherever you go, you'll top all the rest."

Qoheleth *says* the opposite. He concluded that we will feel like we've lived. Like we've accomplished things. Like we've gone places. But in reality, we are stuck in an endless cycle. There are things we have to come to understand. One is that we will *never* be fulfilled. *"All things are full of weariness and man cannot utter it. The eye is not satisfied with seeing, nor the ear filled with hearing." (1:8)* In other words, if we are stuck in an endless cycle of life, and if everything is, at best, temporary, then we will never be truly satisfied.

Have you ever watched a good movie? Have you ever enjoyed a good meal or seen a beautiful sunset? They satisfy for a little while, but then you have to do it again, because it does not last. You enjoy the meal, but you have to eat again. You enjoy the sunset, but the memory fades, and you want to see it again. When your favorite sports team wins the championship, are you satisfied forever? Or do you want to see them win again next year?

Life is like a Chinese food buffet. We can eat all we want, but an hour later we will be hungry again. If we are honest about the human condition, we will always want more. A little more money. A better job. A longer vacation. One more fish. One more game. One more drink. One more chance. We have deceived ourselves into thinking that we will eventually get enough.

But we never do.

In Frank Capra's classic 1947 movie, *It's a Wonderful Life*, George Bailey struggles with living in his small hometown. He feels like if he could just have something big, if he could discover something important, then life would have meaning. George assumed he would find meaning somewhere other than where he was. That is the human condition. We are seldom satisfied with what we have.

"Is there anything of which it is said, 'See, this is new.'" (Ecc 1:10)

Qoheleth says the future is simply the past repeated. Now this does not mean that there are no new inventions. He was not saying there was never going to be an *iPhone*, or the *Keurig* coffee maker. Rather, Qoheleth is saying that in the past there was war, and in the future there will be war. In the past, children disobeyed their parents. In the future, children will disobey their parents. In the past, marriages struggled. In the future, marriages will struggle. The future is simply a repeat of the past. The same song. Different verse. It only feels different because it is happening to you. So, in that sense, we will never actually experience anything new.

We will eventually be forgotten. *"There is no remembrance of former things, nor will there be any remembrance of later things yet to be among those who will come after."* *(1:11)* You can think you are going to be different. You are going to make a difference. But Qoheleth would say that's not true. You, like everyone else, will be born, you will get on the treadmill of life, and you will die.

Years later no one will even remember your name. As Mark Twain said:

A myriad of men are born; they labor and sweat and struggle for bread; they squabble and scold and fight; they scramble for little mean advantages over each other. Age creeps upon them; infirmities follow; shames and humiliations bring down their prides and their vanities. Those they love are taken from them and the joy of life is turned to aching grief. The burden of pain, care, misery, grows heavier year by year. At length ambition is dead; pride is dead; vanity is dead; longing for release is in their place. It comes at last - the only un-poisoned gift ever had for them - and they vanish from a world where they were of no consequence; where they achieved nothing; where they were a mistake and a failure and a foolishness; where they have left no sign that they have existed – a world which will lament them a day and forget them forever. Then another myriad takes their place and copies all they did and goes along the same profitless road and vanishes as they vanished - to make room for another and another and a million other myriads to follow the same arid path through the same desert and accomplish what the first myriad and all the myriads that came after it accomplished - nothing!" [emphasis added]

Take for example celebrities like Robin Williams. When they die, they stay in the news for a day or two, but the story fades in the shadow of the *next* story. Recently there was a death of a long-standing supreme court justice. On the very day she died, many of the newscasts are already discussing how she will be replaced, who will replace her, and how soon? ON THE DAY OF HER PASSING! That is Qoheleth's point!

Benjamin Cheever had been an editor at *Reader's Digest* for more than a decade when he decided to follow in the footsteps of his famous father, John Cheever, and write a novel. Working in his Pleasantville, New York home, he wrote a book called *The Plagiarist.* It was published in 1992. Like most first novels, it was somewhat autobiographical. It featured a magazine that strongly resembled his famous employer, and the main character's father was an alcoholic and self-destructive literary success.

In the book, one character worked for a company that sold shampoo. There was a discussion about what might be done to increase sales. He came up with an idea—something simple, yet revolutionary. Add just one word to the label on each bottle: *Repeat.*

When that change was made and the product instructions were amended to say, *"Lather – Rinse – Repeat,"* sales went up dramatically.

Ecclesiastes reminds us that creation is in a perpetual *lather-rinse-repeat* cycle.

All of this is to say that if you will just be honest with yourself, you will rationally conclude that life is an endless cycle, in which you will never be satisfied, you will never experience anything that is truly new, and you ultimately will not be remembered. So, in light of these brutal facts, just try your best to enjoy what you can while you can until it is over.

But is this all there is? Qoheleth is rational, but does he go far enough? As a follower of Christ, how would you respond to such a definitive conclusion? Would you have an answer? Would you quote your mom, or your dad—or your church? What would be the right response?

First, we have to ask ourselves, is Qoheleth correct in his assessment of life? I would say that he is absolutely right. The evidence is irrefutable. This is precisely the conclusion you should draw. But it really doesn't matter if I think he is right. There is someone with more authority than me who also agrees with Qoheleth. His name is Paul. The Apostle Paul.

In Romans 8:20 Paul said, *"For the creation was subjected to futility."* The word, futility, is the Greek translation of the Hebrew word, *vanity*. So, in Romans chapter eight, Paul's use of the word, futility, is the same as what Qoheleth used in Ecclesiastes—vanity. Romans 8:20-22 says, *"For the creation was subjected to futility, not willingly, but because of Him, who subjected it in hope; because the creation itself also will be delivered from the bondage of corruption into the glorious liberty of the children of God. For we know that the whole creation groans and labors with birth pangs together until now."*

The Apostle Paul is in complete agreement with Qoheleth! Creation is caught in an endless cycle of corruption. BUT! Paul says something Qoheleth does not. In Romans 8:11, he said, *"But if the Spirit of Him who raised Jesus from the dead dwells in you, He who raised Christ from the dead will also give life to your mortal bodies through His Spirit who dwells in you."*

Qoheleth says life is caught in an endless cycle, and therefore, is meaningless. Paul agrees…to a point. Paul agrees that life is a cycle of birth and death. Of seasons coming and going. *Groundhog Day.* Lather-Rinse-Repeat. But Paul knows something Qoheleth did not know.

Imagine the following conversation between Qoheleth and the Apostle Paul:

Qoheleth: I believe death makes life an endless cycle.
Paul: I completely agree. Life is caught in a curse, an endless cycle of corruption.
Qoheleth: Amen! That's why life is meaningless.
Paul: Yes, but what if there was someone who broke the cycle? What if, into this endless cycle of humanity, there

was a human who was born, died, BUT CAME BACK
TO LIFE!

Qoheleth: If that were the case, then meaning in life could
only be found in the one who broke the endless cycle.

Paul: Well, Qoheleth, that's the good news of the gospel.
THERE IS ONE WHO DID. His name is Jesus!

You see, Qoheleth says the grave makes life meaningless. The
gospel says an empty grave gives life meaning! Jesus broke the cycle,
and, therefore, he is the only one who will give meaning to our routine
lives. When we feel stuck, in a marriage, in a job, in a routine, and we
struggle to find meaning in our lives, there is good news. There is hope
in the one who broke the cycle.

Chapter Seven

"Knowledge Has Limits"

"*I, the preacher, have been king over Israel in Jerusalem, and I applied my heart to seek and to search out by wisdom all that is done under heaven. It's an unhappy business that God has given to the children of man to be busy with. I've seen everything that's done under the sun, and behold, all is vanity, and a striving after wind. 'What is crooked cannot be made straight, what is lacking cannot be counted.' I said in my heart,' I have acquired great wisdom surpassing all who were over Jerusalem before me, and my heart has had great experience of wisdom and knowledge.' I applied my heart to know wisdom and to know madness and folly. I perceived that this also is but a striving after wind. 'For in much wisdom is much vexation, and he who increases knowledge increases sorrow.'"* Ecclesiastes 1:12-18

D aniel Tammet is, without question, one of the smartest people alive. In addition to his autism, Daniel has savant syndrome, but it is his "disability" (as some would call it) that has enabled him to astound. You see, Daniel has an extraordinary memory, particularly as it relates to numbers and language.

For example, on March 14th 2004, when Daniel was 25 years old, he broke the European record for reciting the endless sequence of numbers known as pi. You remember pi from school, right? It is the ratio of a circle's circumference to its diameter. Daniel did this for 5 hours, 9 minutes, and 24 seconds. To put that into perspective, that's 20,514 digits from memory, without error. He might still be reciting as I write this had he not gotten tired. That's because what kept Daniel from continuing was not making a mistake, but becoming physically and mentally exhausted. I can relate, it's hard enough for me to eat pie for even an hour!

As if that wasn't amazing enough, if you give Daniel any date in history, he'll tell you what day of the week it was on. If you tell him, for instance, August 14th 1911, he'll say Wednesday. Or May 17th 1957, he'll yawn and say, Friday.

How about math skills? Ask Daniel to multiply 31 by 31 by 31 by 31. And Daniel will quickly inform you that the answer is 923,521.

It's not just calculating. His gift of memory is stunning. Briefly show him a long numerical sequence, like 914-1934-217-1844-32-2381, and he'll recite it right back to you, without error.

In addition to his impressive ability with numbers, Daniel is also amazing with languages. He knows eight different languages, one of which is Icelandic. Why? Why would you want to know Icelandic? Daniel decided to learn it because he was invited to do an interview in Iceland and figured he might as well learn their language. He learned it in less than a week. He's so brilliant, he's even invented his own language known as Manti. All of this and more is what has given Daniel the nickname 'The Brain Man.'

As you can imagine, Daniel's knowledge has gained him a lot of notoriety, fame, a good career in writing books and speaking. He's helped to make breakthroughs in mathematics and brain research. There is, however, one thing all his knowledge has not given him: Peace. In his book, *Born on a Blue Day*, which is a memoir of his life, Daniel describes an occasion when he first realized there was a limit to his knowledge. Daniel said, *"I still remember lying on the floor of my room, staring at the ceiling. I was trying to picture the universe in my head, to have a concrete understanding of what everything was, to know reality. In my mind, I traveled to the edge of existence, wondering what I would find, searching. In that moment, I felt unwell and I could feel my heart beating inside me. For the first time, I realized that thought and logic had limits, and can only take a person so far. This realization frightened me. It took me a long time to come to terms with it."*

Think about that. Here is a man with extraordinary knowledge. He can recite pi for over five hours. He can learn a foreign language in less than one week, and yet, when he tries to make sense of life, he realizes knowledge can only take him so far, and it frightens him.

That's exactly what Qoheleth discovered as well, except he is even smarter and wiser than Daniel. *"I, the preacher, have been king over Israel in Jerusalem." (1:12)* Qoheleth is saying, "I am a king with no equal. If there is somebody of my status, if there's somebody at my level of life, they should be able to find meaning in life. If somebody has the resources that I have, if somebody is in the position of life that I'm in, they should be able to make sense out of life." Yet, with all these resources at his fingertips, Qoheleth set out to find meaning in knowledge, *"And I applied my heart to seek and to search out by wisdom, all that's done under the sun." (1:13)*

Qoheleth turns over every rock, he questions every premise. He dedicated himself completely to finding meaning in life through knowledge and wisdom. Of course, it makes sense that he would start with knowledge. After all, if you are consumed with the question of meaning, the best place to start is knowledge.

In my research for this book, I came across a study done at Johns Hopkins University involving 8000 college students across 48 universities. They were asked, "When you get out of college, what's the most important thing that you want? What's the number one thing in life that you desire the most once you leave college?"

What they expected to hear were things like money, a job, marriage, career, but 75% of the 8000 students said their first goal after college was to find *purpose*. You see, that's what humans want. Nobody wants to get to the end of their life and say, "I missed what life was all about." Ultimately, everyone searches for this. Qoheleth devoted himself fully, 24/7, to finding meaning in life through knowledge.

"I said in my heart, I have acquired great wisdom, surpassing all who were over Jerusalem before me, and my heart has had great experience of wisdom, and knowledge." *(1:16)* Qoheleth became the top student in the class. He read every book, he graduated with every degree, he's got a GED, a MD, and a PhD. He had so much knowledge he was able to say, "There was not anybody before me, who maintained or obtained the status of knowledge that I have." [This is why I think this is an allusion to Solomon.]

Remember in 1 Kings 3 when God said to Solomon, "Make your request?" Instead of asking for riches, Solomon asked for wisdom. God said, "Because you asked for wisdom instead of riches, I'll give you both." As a result, Solomon gained the highest level of knowledge, of intellect, of wisdom that you could possibly gain under the sun. Yet, it didn't answer all the questions of life.

We do the same thing. All of us, in some way, look to knowledge to provide value, meaning, significance, or worth to our lives. We do this in small ways and big ways. Some of us have thought, "If I can just get that position in that company, then I will be valued." Or as a student, "If I could only be accepted in that school, then I'll be accepted. If I can only go to that prestigious academic institution, then I will matter."

As a former professor at 3 different academic institutions, and someone with a Ph.D., I know full well how people look to knowledge to answer their questions. Maybe for you it is not an institutional search, maybe it is far more practical. Maybe you watch shows like Jeopardy. Or play board games like Trivial Pursuit. Or watch movies like *Good Will Hunting* or *A Beautiful Mind*, or *The Accountant*.

That's why I loved researching Daniel Tammet. There's something in me that loves knowledge and thinks, "Man, I wish I could do that. I wish I were as smart as he is." Do you like being the smartest person in the room? Maybe you're thinking, "I don't know what that feels like." Sure, you do.

You know that feeling you get inside when a topic comes up that you're an expert in and, all of a sudden, you can contribute to the conversation? Someone brings up cars. Hey, I know cars! Or theology. I know theology! Or sports? I can sure talk sports! Or cooking. Now we're in my wheelhouse! Or someone asks about financing. I know about that! You see? Inside, even if only in a small way, you feel like, now, in *this* conversation, I matter. I can contribute.

If none of these examples have applied to you, what about this? How do you feel about *not* knowing? How do you feel when you are in conversations and you have no idea what they are talking about? You feel like one big zero! Why? Because if you had the knowledge then you would matter.

One way or another we all look to knowledge to give meaning to life.

Knowledge is like a warm blanket that makes us feel good at night, because it gives us a sense of control. It's why we can't stand it when somebody says, "I've got something really important I want to talk to you about, but we'll talk about it next week." We say, "No, we won't. We're talking about it now." Why? We've got to know. There's something about knowing that makes us feel like we matter. There's a significance there.

How many of us as parents have told our children, "Get good grades in school so that you can go to a good college. Get a good degree, because that'll get you a good job, and that will lead to a better life." Probably *every* parent. Why? What's the mentality? It's that knowledge is what will get us to the good life.

My point is everybody is like Qoheleth. We think knowledge can provide meaning in life. Knowledge, if we could just get enough of it, would answer life's ultimate problems. Here's the clincher to why I know this is true for all of us. It was at the core of the fall of humanity. Remember in Genesis 3.

"But the serpent said to the woman, you will not surely die, for God knows when you eat of it, your eyes will be opened, and you will be like God..." How so? *"...knowing good and evil. So when the woman saw that the tree was good for food, and that it was a delight to the eyes, and that the tree was to be desired to make one wise, she took of its fruit and ate, and she also gave some to her husband who was with her, and he ate." (Gen 3:4)* What was going on in the Garden? If I could just know, then I could be god, god of my life, god at my job, god at my school. If I could just know, then I could be in control, I could reign—and we've been eating that fruit ever since.

All of us, in little ways and in big ways, like Qoheleth, look to wisdom and knowledge, saying, "If I can just get enough of it, then I can make sense out of life." So Qoheleth reads every book, gets every degree, and here's his conclusion: *"I have seen everything that is done under the sun, and behold, all is vanity and a striving after the wind." (Ecc 1:14)* And, *"I applied my heart to know wisdom and to know madness and folly. I perceived that this also is but striving after wind." (Ecc 1:17)* He says it's meaningless. It's like chasing the wind.

After all his reading, after all his studying, after all of his degrees, after all his knowledge and wisdom, he ends up like Daniel Tammet, lying on the floor and staring at the ceiling, dismayed that his knowledge won't take him far enough. This is where Qoheleth ends up, and he is more than willing to give you his reasons for why he found knowledge to be meaningless. That is, if you still have the courage to engage...

Chapter Eight

"Right Question, Wrong Answer"

I f you are reading this, I assume you are still willing to engage with Qoheleth's quest to find meaning in life. As we have discussed, the first thing Qoheleth pursued, in order to find the answers to life's ultimate questions, was knowledge. But that proved to be vanity. Knowledge is very important and useful *in* life, but it can't bring meaning *to* life. Quohelth would now like to tell you why. In fact, he has 5 reasons why knowledge cannot provide meaning in life.

"For in much wisdom is much vexation, and he who increases knowledge increases sorrow." (Ecc 1:18) Rather than freeing you from your problems, knowledge often opens your eyes to more problems. In most things in life, the more you know, the more you wish you didn't.

Ignorance, on many issues, really is bliss because the more you know about life, the more you know how absurd it is.

Take, for example, politics. The more you know about politics...the more you know how corrupt it can be, right? In my experience, most people who get really involved in politics either eventually walk away disillusioned by what they discover and no longer want to be involved, or they become so one-sided they can no longer have an adult conversation. More knowledge didn't solve problems, it is just created more.

Or theology.... I've dedicated my life to the study of theology. I have a degree in theology, and here is what my study of theology has taught me: The more I know, the more I realize how much I don't know. The more I understand about God, the clearer understanding I get of his incalculable immensity and richness, and the more overwhelmed I am by how much more there is to know about God.

Or church? For many people they viewed church as a peaceful place where people hold hands and everyone gets along. But the more people are involved in church the more they realize it is full of sinners, there is conflict among members, politics behind the scenes, and many other things they didn't really want to *know* about church.

My point is, there are all kinds of areas where more knowledge actually leads to more anxiety. It increases sorrow, not removes it. It also happens on a practical level. For example, rollercoasters. When I was a kid, I would get on any roller coaster. It didn't matter how fast it went, how far it dropped, how many loops it made. Now, I get on one and I'm terrified. I would just as soon keep my two feet on the ground. My son says, "Let's ride," and I'm like, "Let's not." I know too much now. I've gained too much knowledge to be so carefree. I have responsibilities. I have children. My knowledge of life means I get really nervous when I get on a roller coaster. Knowledge can't ultimately satisfy because knowledge in most areas leaves you saying, "I wish I didn't know that."

Secondly, Qoheleth would say that knowledge is great but it won't give you security in life. *"Then I saw that there is more gain in wisdom than in folly, as there is more gain in light than in darkness. The wise person has his eyes in his head, but the fool walks in darkness. And yet I perceived that the same event happens to all of them. Then I said in my heart, 'What happens to the fool will happen to me also. Why then have I been so very wise? And I said in my heart that this also is vanity."* (Ecc 2:13)

Wisdom is helpful. Wisdom is a good thing. It's better than being a moron, right? Yes, but wisdom doesn't make your life any better. The heart attack doesn't stop to ask if you graduated college. The drunk driver doesn't swerve out of the way of smart people. Cancer's not going to stop and ask you your IQ score. The hurricane doesn't care if you graduated from Harvard or the local junior college. Knowledge will help you a lot, but it won't guarantee you a thing. Knowledge is good and it is certainly better than the alternative, but it does not make your life secure.

Thirdly, knowledge cannot be sustained. *"For of the wise as of the fool there is no enduring remembrance, seeing that in the days to come all will have been long forgotten."* (2:16) Even if you are the best speaker on the planet, and many people come to hear you, most walk away and forget everything you said! Think about your favorite class in school.

The one you excelled in the most (and recess or lunch doesn't count). Now, can you restate *ALL* the content you learned? Or *any* part of it verbatim? Doubtful. That's with your favorite one. Imagine the ones you didn't like. You may remember a couple of principles, you may even remember the teacher's name, but you have forgotten most of what you've learned. Knowledge can't and will not be sustained. This becomes even more challenging the older you become.

In addition, knowledge won't keep you safe. *"How the wise dies just like the fool!" (Ecc 2:16)* What's Qoheleth saying? You can outsmart a lot of people, but you can't outsmart death. Einstein didn't. He is the one we compare everyone to! "Well, I'm no Einstein." Qoheleth would argue, what's the point of being really, really wise, if you can't even outsmart death?

The final reason Qohelth gives for why knowledge, while good, can't provide meaning in life is that knowledge provides no ultimate solutions. *"If the serpent bites before it is charmed, there is no advantage to the charmer." (10:11)* If you had the wisdom to train a snake [and I have no idea why you'd want such wisdom,], that wisdom and training won't help you if the serpent bites you. In other words, it doesn't bring lasting solutions.

All the knowledge in the world won't bring your spouse back. All the educational degrees will not answer why you had three miscarriages. You can have a lot of knowledge, but when it comes to life's biggest questions, it simply isn't enough.

This is very reality that led Qoheleth to say, *"I hated life." (2:17)*

That's rock bottom. Why did Qoheleth hit rock bottom? Because what is worse than never getting what your heart desires is getting what your heart desires *and realizing it doesn't satisfy you*. Pursuing knowledge hoping it will answer all your questions only to gain knowledge and still be left with questions.

Qoheleth ends up just like Daniel Tammet. He's lying on the ground and staring at the ceiling, saying, "Knowledge hasn't taken me far enough." Tim Keller writes, "Most people spend their lives trying to make their heart's fondest dreams come true. I mean, isn't that what life is all about, the pursuit of happiness? We search endlessly for ways to acquire the things we desire, and we're willing to sacrifice much to achieve them, but we never imagine that getting our heart's deepest desires might be the worst thing that could ever happen."

As a result, Qoheleth puts together a proverb that summarizes his conclusion, *"What is crooked cannot be made straight, and what is lacking cannot be counted." (1:15)* In other words, life is a question that cannot be answered. Life is bent, it's broken, and it cannot be made straight.

Life, if you are really honest, doesn't make sense. It's why when you're at the grocery store, the other line always moves faster. As soon as your hands are covered in grease, your nose will itch; as soon as you buy it, it will go on sale somewhere else. The probability of someone watching you is directly related to the stupidity of the act. Be assured, if the shoe fits, it's probably ugly. Life, as awesome as it is, often makes no sense at all.

Qoheleth is willing to take this one step further. A step most non-believers are willing to take, but most believers are afraid to. Qoheleth says if you want to look at who is to blame for this puzzle called life that clearly has missing pieces, this riddle that can't be solved, this crooked thing that can't be straightened, look no further than God Himself! *"It is an unhappy business that God has given to the children of man to be busy with."* *(2:13)* This pursuit that ends up in no answers is what God has given the children of man to do. God has created life this way. God has made it so that there are no answers to life's ultimate questions or, at least, He has hidden them in a place where you can't find them. This is not the only place in Ecclesiastes where he states something like this:

> *"Consider the work of God: who can make straight...,"* [do you see the parallel?] *"...who can make straight what he has made crooked? In the day of prosperity be joyful."* Enjoy the good days while you can. *"In the day of adversity consider: God has made the one as well as the other,"* [and why has he made the crooked day and the joyful day?] *"so that man may not find out anything that will be after him."* *(7:13)*

> *"When I applied my heart to know wisdom, and to see the business that is done on earth, how neither day nor night do one's eyes see sleep, then I saw all the work of God, that man cannot find out the work that is done under the sun. However, much man may toil in seeking, he will not find it out."* *(Ecc 8:16)*

If we don't like the way the store is arranged, blame the manager. If we don't like the way the team is playing, blame the coach. If we don't like the way life is ordered, guess what? Look no further than the One who created life.

What is Qoheleth's suggestion? What should you do when you realize that knowledge, while important, has limits? Here is his advice: *"Be not overly righteous, and do not make yourself too wise. Why should you destroy yourself?"* You've got to laugh, at some point, to stay sane, right? *"Be not overly wicked, neither be a fool. Why should you die before your time?" (7:16)* In other words, don't be an idiot, because, after all, you've got to have *some* knowledge to make it through life. Go to school, learn, because you need knowledge, but don't know too much, because it will drive you crazy. You need to know enough to get through life but don't know so much that you lose your mind.

Is that good advice? It is the wisdom literature section of the Bible. So, what would you say to Qoheleth if he laid out the reasons above. How would you answer a man who is renowned for his wisdom and knowledge, drawing this rational, conclusion about life? Here's what I would say, "Qohelth, you are exactly right. But there is something you are missing..."

Chapter Nine

"Principles or a Person?"

Qoheleth is right that meaning in life cannot be found in wisdom and knowledge, if you believe that wisdom and knowledge is nothing more than a set of principles and proverbs. But wisdom is more than that. In fact, meaning in life, true meaning in life, can only be found in wisdom. Let me explain.

The Apostle Paul wrote twice to the church in Corinth. Their Greco/Roman culture told them that meaning is found in human philosophy, human wisdom, just like Qoheleth and many, many people assume. Paul wrote to that church in that context, and said, *"For the word of the cross is folly* [Ecclesiastes' language] *to those who are perishing, but to us who are being saved it is the power of God. For it is written, 'I will destroy the wisdom of the wise, and the discernment of the discerning I will thwart.'" (1 Cor 1:18-19)* Then beginning in verse 26, *"For consider your calling, brothers: not many of you were wise according to worldly standards, not many were powerful, not many of noble birth. But God chose what is foolish in the world to shame the wise; God chose what is weak in the world to shame the strong; God chose what is low and despised in the world, so that is no human being might boast in the presence of God."* Then, in verse 30, *"And because of him you are in Christ Jesus, who became to us wisdom from God...."*

According to the Apostle Paul, true wisdom and knowledge is not found in college, textbooks, or even life experience. Wisdom is the person of Christ. Jesus is the Logos that is from the beginning.

This means that until we stop seeing wisdom as a set of principles and proverbs, and start seeing wisdom as a person, you will never make sense out of life. That changes everything. Qoheleth was right to say that meaning is found in wisdom. He was just looking in the wrong place.

True wisdom is found on a cross and in a now-empty grave. It is the person of Jesus Christ. That truth is the good news of the gospel. There are two very important implications that come from this.

To embrace the wisdom of Christ you must be willing to be seen as foolish to the world. If wisdom is a person, and you're following that person, and that person, Jesus Christ, is all about the kingdom of God, then as you live in the kingdom of man, they're going to think you're crazy. They're going to say things like, "How can you give that way? How can you forgive like that? Why would you spend your time serving *those people*? How can you approach marriage like that? How can you respond to suffering with that kind of faith?" In other words, you're walking in wisdom, wisdom whom the world doesn't recognize. The irony here is that when you discover true Wisdom, the person of Jesus Christ, your life starts to make sense while at the same time your life makes no sense to others!

Life will only make sense when you have discovered the foolishness of following Jesus. As long as you keep trying to live this life according to the wisdom of the world, you will continue to end up on the floor and staring at the ceiling, knowing that your knowledge didn't take you far enough.

Now, some folks, particularly young people in school, might say at this point, "Sweet. I'm not going to class tomorrow. It's just following Jesus, right? It's not about college, it's about Jesus. The man with a Ph.D. said so." That would be taking things out of context.

When you see wisdom as person, then all pursuit of knowledge is an effort to know and glorify Him. If all truth is God's truth wherever it is found, as Augustine said, then go, learn, study, think to the glory of God. It's a reversal of Eden, because you're not looking to knowledge to become God. You're looking to knowledge as a means of worshiping God. Whether that's science, farming, sewing, or whatever topic it is, you approach that topic as a means of knowing and glorifying God, which ought to make you the best student in the class.

When you understand that wisdom is a person, it changes why you go to school, it changes why you read a book, because you don't turn your brain off to worship God. The approach to life is not, "Learn as little as you can." It is, "I want to learn as much as I can, not because I think it will provide meaning, but because I've already found meaning in Jesus." Qoheleth was right. Wisdom is absolutely the key to meaning in life. He just didn't see, as the fullness of revelation had occurred, that wisdom is a person.

Qoheleth is also right about the fact that God has made life so you can't find the answer. I didn't say God has made life so there is no answer. I'm saying, God has arranged life so that you can't find the answer on your own. *"If any of you lacks wisdom, let him ask God, who gives generously to all without reproach, and it will be given him." (James 1:5)* James didn't say ask and you will gain wisdom,. He says *ask and it will be given.* By and from God.

The meaning of life is found, not by becoming wise enough to figure out your life, but by realizing you're not wise enough to figure it out, and therefore must look to God. In other words, wisdom is found, not by self-effort, but by surrender. God loves you so much, he wants you frustrated by your lack of answers under the sun so that you will run to him for answers, and surrender by faith to the Son. Yes, he set it up where you can't figure out the answers because you weren't designed to figure out the answers. You were designed to surrender to a holy God, who would then give you the answers. At some point, you must end up where Qoheleth ended up, where Daniel Tammet ended up, namely realizing your knowledge is not enough.

He wants you there so that you'll finally understand where meaning is found in a fallen world—in the person of Jesus Christ.

I'm asking you today, would you be "foolish" enough to stop living life according to your own effort, according to your own knowledge? Would you surrender, by faith, to Jesus Christ? Because, if you will be willing to do that, it would be the wisest decision you've ever made.

Chapter Ten

"Party Like It's 1999."

W hat artist broke the record for the most consecutive weeks at number one in the modern music era? Not only that, but when their second song debuted, it debuted at number two, which gave them the number one and number two spot at the same time, something that only 11 artists have ever accomplished. They held the top spots for 26 consecutive weeks, making them one of only two artists who have ever stayed at the top of the charts for half of a calendar year. Do you know the artist?

If your guess is the *Black Eyed Peas*, you got it right. Their song that was at number one for 14 consecutive weeks is a song called, "*I Got A Feeling*." If you have never heard the song, the lyrics go like this: "*Tonight's the night, let's live it up. I got my money, Let's spend it up...I know that we'll have a ball if we get down and go out and just lose it all."* Listen to this language. *"I feel stressed out. I wanna let it go. Let's go way out, spaced out, losing all control. Let's paint the town, We'll shut it down. Let's burn the roof. And then we'll do it again on Monday, Tuesday, Wednesday, Thursday, Friday, Saturday, Saturday to Sunday. Get with us, You know what we say: Party every day. Party every day," right? And then we'll do it again."*

Whether or not you like that song, or even ever heard that song, its success was proof that it resonated strongly with our culture. In fact, *Billboard Magazine* called it, *"An anthem for people trying to escape life's pressures by going out and having a ball."*

Of course, *I've Got A Feeling* was not the first song that ever expressed that desire. *The Beach Boys* said you can have fun, fun, fun. Cindy Lauper said girls just want to have fun. *The Beastie Boys* said you got to fight for your right to party. *KISS* wanted to rock and roll all night and party every day. All Sheryl Crow wanted to do was just have some fun. Justin Timberlake had to dance, dance, dance because, evidently, he can't stop the feeling! Then, of course, there is the late Prince, whose lyrics summarize it the best, *"War is all around us. My mind says prepare to fight. So, if I gotta die, I'm gonna listen to my body tonight. They say 2000, zero, zero party over, Oops, out of time. So, tonight we're gonna party like it's 1999."* Had Prince not written that song, I'm quite certain Qoheleth would have.

What's the message? The message is, if we're all going to die anyway, if there are ultimately no answers to the questions of life, then party. Go out and have a ball. Live it up while you can. Then do it again! That's where Qoheleth, in his search for meaning in life, turns next.

"I said in my heart, 'Come now, I will test you with pleasure; enjoy yourself.'" *(2:1)* Anything that looks good, that feels good, that's pleasurable, he was going after it all.

Does it not make sense to turn to pleasure after falling short with knowledge? *"...I applied my heart to know wisdom and to know madness and folly. I perceived that this also is but a striving after wind. For in much wisdom is much vexation, and he who increases knowledge increases sorrow. I said in my heart, 'Come now. I will test you with pleasure.'"* Here's the shift: since knowledge didn't ultimately provide the answers to the questions I'm asking, I will try pleasure. That's insightful because once you lose your search for objective truth, the natural slide is to do whatever is right in your own eyes.

That's true for a country. That's true for a culture. That's true for a church, for a family, for an individual. When you lose an objective reason for living, you will find a subjective reason for living. When you lose a grasp on truth, then the natural next step is "I'll do whatever I want." Anything goes.

This is American culture. Let me take you quickly through this journey over the last five decades. In the 1950s, there was a loss of innocence. World War II was over, the population was growing rapidly. An entertainment explosion took place. Who became the ultimate definer of values and mindset in American culture? Hollywood. Hollywood began to shape the American mindset.

Enter the 1960s. In the '60s, America lost a sense of authority. There were protests in Woodstock and riots in LA, Detroit,

Memphis, and Chicago. There were two major assassinations, namely JFK and Martin Luther King Jr. The objective sense of authority was questioned and discounted in the counter-culture, and that anti-authority attitude continued.

Then came the 1970s and the belief in real love was lost. Drugs and sex mushroomed (pun intended). They'd always been there, but now they dominated the culture. People searching for love were settling for sex, and the divorce culture exploded.

What did America lose in the '80s? We lost all sense of style. If you had a pair of parachute pants, burn them in Jesus name! What were we thinking?

Ok, that's not really what America lost in the 1980s. What we lost was a sense of values. There was the meteoric rise of technology and wealth. Materialism became a major, *major* focus. One of the most successful movies in the '80s was *Wall Street*. What was the message of that movie? "Greed is good." Values were seriously eroded in the culture during that decade.

In the 1990s, the erosion continued. The sense of community continued to erode. There were school shootings, more riots in LA, the whole country was shocked by the Oklahoma City Bombing.

The new millennium began with a major loss of confidence, a deep loss of any sense of security. Y2K panicked everyone. Then 9/11 happened and we entered this age of terrorism. At first it was enemies from outside the country, and as a result we banded together to resist and defend. Now, we are experiencing domestic terrorism, leaving everyone afraid and insecure. Is it any wonder that so many people are desperately searching for hope, for relief, for escape?

Qoheleth decides (like just about every other person at some point in their life), "I'm gonna throw a party. I'm going to enjoy myself." He throws a party that makes any party you've ever been to look like a preschool birthday party.

"And whatever my eyes desired I did not keep from them. I kept my heart from no pleasure, for my heart found pleasure in all my toil." (2:10) Remember this is a man of great resources. This is a king figure. This is a Solomon figure. He has all the resources necessary.

Qoheleth didn't merely dabble in pleasure, he didn't just dip a toe in to test the waters. He gave himself over to four primary expressions of pleasure:

Laughter. *"I said of laughter...."* Qoheleth hires Larry the Cable Guy, Will Ferrell, and Jim Gaffigan and brings Bob Hope back from the dead. He watches all day marathons of *Dumb and Dumber* and *The Tonight Show* with Johnny Carson, and Live from Jerusalem, it's Saturday Night. He laughs it up.

Have you ever had one of those moments when you laughed so hard you cried, when you laughed so hard that your stomach hurt? We love to laugh, don't we? Laughter is a great thing—but it can also be the dark cave of a troubled soul. Think John Belushi, Richard Pryor, Robin Williams, and one of my favorites, Chris Farley. All the laughter in the world could not give them peace. Laughter is a good thing. It is a gift from God, but if we try to turn it into something that provides *meaning* to our lives, it becomes the dark cave of a troubled soul.

Wine. *"I searched with my heart how to cheer my body with wine."* From the cheap beer at NASCAR, to Tennessee whiskey, to the elegant wines of California, Qoheleth tried them all. He even had his own vineyards. He tried all the best wine one could possibly have.

Wine is a good thing, but wine can also be the dark cave of a troubled soul. Dennis Wilson from the Beach Boys, is an example (of many) of a life that spun out-of-control due to alcohol. His life really reflected their music: fast cars, easy women, perfect waves, and endless summers. That is, it did until they found his body in 13 feet of murky water in a Marina Del Ray boat slip. You know why? Because at the age of 39, he was dead after a heavy day of drinking. He had checked himself into a 21 detox program months earlier with a .28 blood alcohol level and traces of cocaine. They said that at that point in his life he was drinking, at a minimum, a fifth of Vodka a day. Here's what one of his ex-wives said, "It hurts to see people you love go down. Dennis was empty inside. He tried to fill that need with anything he could." This is not about wine being a bad thing. It's about the fact that it can become the dark cave of a troubled soul.

Music. *"I got singers, both men and women…."* This guy is so rich, he hires his favorite bands to come and play. He doesn't have Spotify yet, so he hires Survivor to be waiting in his bedroom, so that as soon as he wakes up, he can start the day with *The Eye of the Tiger.* He flies in Chris Tomlin for his quiet time. Do you love music? I do. I love good music: jazz, classic, country. It's such a gift from God. Sometimes songs say things our mouths can't.

Sometimes music is the dark cave of a troubled soul. I remember getting the phone call. It was seven o'clock on a Wednesday night, and the voice on the other end said, "Your grandfather has passed." I walked into my room, put my headphones on, and tried to drown the pain with music.

Sex. "...*and many concubines, the delight of the sons of man.*" One of my favorite theologians, the late Waylon Jennings, said this "*The only two things in life that make it worth living are guitars tuned good and firm-feelin' women.*" Qoheleth could have written that song.

This is clearly a parallel to Solomon. King Solomon had 700 wives. Not only 700 wives, but also 300 concubines. That's 1,000 women. He's the Wilt Chamberlain of the ancient near East. He's not looking for Mrs. Right. He's looking for Mrs. Right Now.

Sex is a good thing. Sex was designed by God. God is the one that put two people in a garden and said, "Be fruitful and multiply." It is God's design. Sex can be the dark cave of a troubled soul. It's easy to think that maybe if I could have a woman in my life, if I can just have a man in my life, then I can make sense out of it.

Could God's Word written over two millennia ago in Ecclesiastes be any more relevant for today? We do this all the time. You and I look to indulgence and pleasure for meaning. The reason we do not go to this extreme is because most of us don't have the resources. Look at the celebrity culture, the "elites," those who do have the resources, and you'll find the same life.

Here's how I know that we *all* look to pleasure and indulgence to try to make sense out of life, to try to find meaning.

We overeat. We overeat a LOT. The National Institute of Health says more than two-thirds of adults, that is 70%, are overweight. More than a third, 35%, are obese. Comedian Jim

Gaffigan says, "What's the big deal about Thanksgiving...we overeat...yeah, but we do that every day. The only difference between Thanksgiving and every other day is that, on Thanksgiving, you're doing it with people you don't like."

We're oversexed. The porn industry is a $15 billion industry in the US and $100 billion worldwide. At one point, pornography had larger revenues than Microsoft, Google, Amazon, e-bay, Yahoo, Apple, and Netflix *combined*.

We overspend. The total consumer debt in America is $3.4 trillion. The average person has over $10,300 in credit card debt—and that's just credit card debt.

The point is simply this: Self-indulgence is the American way of life. This is not just an America problem. It's a human problem. Back in Genesis 3:4 the Scripture says, "*But the serpent said to the woman, 'You will not surely die. For God knows that when you eat of it your eyes will be opened, and you will be like God, knowing good and evil.' So when the woman saw that the tree was good for food, [here it comes] and that it was a delight to the eyes....*" Sound familiar? The reality is, humanity has been enjoying the pleasures of that fruit ever since.

Chapter Eleven

"The Party Never Ends"

T he problem with temporary pleasures is that, as great as they are, as enjoyable as they can be, they don't last. That's why they won't and can't provide meaning. Pleasures will give you a great time, but they won't give you a meaningful life. That's what Qoheleth learned in his search for pleasure. When he could not eat any more, when the laughing stopped, the music faded, and the women went home, Qoheleth again said, "It is all vanity." There are 3 reasons why Qoheleth would tell you that while pleasure gives you a great night, it won't give you a purpose.

The first reason is the pleasure is empty. *"I said in my heart, "Come now. I will test you with pleasure; enjoy yourself."" (2:1)* After the biggest buffet, wildest party, and most pleasure money can buy, he says,

"...*and behold, all was vanity and a striving after wind*...." That word "vanity" is often interpreted as "meaningless," which is not wrong, but the actual translation of the word vanity is more like vaporous. There's nothing ultimately there. That is why it is like "striving after wind" is because there is nothing there to catch. It's empty. Fleeting. Here, then gone. His point is to say that pleasure is delightful; it just doesn't last. Pleasure is great; but it evaporates and leaves you empty.

You get the buzz. You feel the passion but rather than satisfying you, what does it do? It leaves you longing for more. You've got to go out the next night. You got to go back to the computer the next day. You got to go back to the relationship again. Why? The very fact that you have to go back out again on (cue the Black-eyed Peas song) *Monday, Tuesday, Wednesday, Thursday, Friday, Saturday, Saturday to Sunday*, and then you have to do it again, and do it again, and do it again is because it's empty. If it satisfied permanently, then you wouldn't have to go back to it. You would not have to "do it again."

When I was growing up in church, I was often told things like, "Don't smoke, go to parties, drink alcohol, or be impure because those things are not fun." This is often the lie religion gives you. I'd think, *not fun?* What planet are you from? It is all kinds of fun. You see, the issue with pursuing these things is not an issue of fun, it is an issue of finding meaning. Qoheleth is not on search for fun. He's on a search for meaning in life. Pleasure will give you all the fun you want, but it will leave you empty in the morning.

Pleasure does not provide meaning also because the demands for pleasure are never satisfied. It's a void that not only doesn't satisfy, but its demands are never satisfied either. That's why we have food addictions and sex addictions and shopping addictions, because the party doesn't last, AND the party itself demands more and more the further down the line you go.

> "*I searched with my heart how to cheer my body with wine—,*" notice the next phrase, "*..my heart still guiding me with wisdom....*" (2:3)

In the Hebrew, this conveys the idea of being dragged along. As he's pursuing pleasure, he still has a nagging thought in his mind that he cannot shake. Wisdom is still there, searching—in computer-speak we'd say there's an app running in the background doing a search for "meaning" even as he's pursuing pleasure. This is ultimately what he's saying—I'm pursuing pleasure, but it still doesn't answer my questions.

The bottle helps me forget for a moment that I lost my son, but it doesn't answer why. Sex gives me the illusion of intimacy, but it still doesn't satisfy my loneliness. I've filled up my house and a storage unit, but it still doesn't answer the deeper questions of my life. That's why he says "it's madness" multiple times; I'm pursuing something I expect to satisfy my need, my questions, but I'm not getting any answers. In other words, pleasure may help you forget, but it will never explain.

A final reason why Qoheleth would say pleasure, while enjoyable, won't give you ultimate meaning is because there is no payoff in the end. *"I said of laughter, 'it is mad,' and of pleasure, 'what use is it?'"* (2:2) There it is, in a nutshell. Why go to all the effort and expense if there's no payoff? Why? Why in the world would you spend all your time, money, and energy on a pursuit that's only going to enslave you? I have never met a porn addict who said, "Porn was worth losing my family." I have never talked to an alcoholic who said, "The drink was worth the destruction of my career." It doesn't gain you anything. What's the point when you run after these things in the name of meaning and all they do is enslave you, and they don't give you anything? You go after it to get something of value, and all it does is take, take, take, take, take, take. It's maddening.

So, here's what Qoheleth has learned. Knowledge didn't work. You need knowledge to get by in life, but it won't give you meaning in life. So, he took the natural next step, "I'll just go after pleasure." Let's party every day. I'll give myself fully to that but that didn't bring meaning either.

What do we say to Qoheleth? What would you tell him? You need to have some kind of answer for him. First, for your own soul and secondly because the world is full of people searching for meaning and they will ask you for an answer. What do you tell someone who has spent their life in the pursuit of pleasure only to come up empty?

The problem is, most Christians and churches give the wrong answer. They resort to religion which usually says something like this, "That's right. Pleasure brings no meaning. So, avoid pleasure. Don't drink. Don't look at porn. Don't listen to rock and roll music. Whatever you do, don't laugh." Religion will give you a list of things to avoid, rules to live by and confirm to. They assume, sadly, that a life absent of pleasure is how to find meaning. If you do anything that feels good, repent. That was the message I was taught in church.

There are serious problems with this approach. First, it's wrong, it's not biblical at all. Secondly, Qoheleth is right, meaning is found in pleasure. You heard me right, you will never find meaning in life a part from pleasure. Let me take you into a very important and insightful moment of the ministry of Jesus.

"On the third day there was a wedding at Cana in Galilee, and the mother of Jesus was there. Jesus also was invited to the wedding with his disciples. When the wine ran out ...." (John 2:1)

Jesus is at a wedding feast, which in the ancient near East was a huge party. A major social gathering and if you ran out of wine it was a social nightmare.

In this situation that is exactly what happened, the wine ran out.

"The mother of Jesus said to him, 'They have no wine.' Jesus said to her, 'Woman, what does this have to do with me? My hour has not yet come.' His mother said to the servants, 'Do whatever he tells you.'"

Mary wants Jesus to do something about this situation. Jesus does.

"Now there were six stone water jars there for the Jewish rites of purification, each holding 20 or 30 gallons. Jesus said to the servants, 'Fill the jars with water.' And they filled them up to the brim. And he said to them, "Now draw some out and take it to the master of the feast. So, they took it. (John 2:6)

"When the master of the feast tasted the water now become wine, and did not know where it came from, (though the servants who had drawn the water knew), the master of the feast called the bridegroom and said to him, 'Everyone serves the good wine first, and when people have drunk freely, then the poor wine."

Why would they be shocked that there was "good wine"? Simple. They would always serve the good wine first because by the end of the night, when people were drinking the bad wine, nobody really cared (or could tell the difference). That's when you bring the cheap stuff out, the local gas station stuff, because by then nobody knows the difference. Notice this. *"But you have kept the good wine, until now. This, the first of his signs, Jesus did at Canaan in Galilee, and manifested his glory. And his disciples believed in him.'"*

What is Jesus doing here? What is the significance of this moment given that it is the first miracle of Jesus? In this life, the party ends. The wine runs out. The music fades. The laughing doesn't last. In the kingdom of God, the party never ends. In fact, what gets served 10,000 years into God's kingdom is even better than the first day. It's keeps getting better and better and better and better. Where is that pleasure found? It's not found in the wine. It's found in the One who has the power to turn water into wine.

Listen, you were created for a party, but that party is a person. It's Jesus.

"You make known to me the path of life; in your presence there is fullness of joy; at your right hand are pleasures forevermore."
(Psalm 16:11)

"How precious is your steadfast love, O God! The children of mankind take refuge in the shadow of your wings."

What do they do?

"They feast on the abundance of your house, and you give them drink from the river of your delights." (Psalm 36:7)

"The thief comes only to steal and kill and destroy. I came that they may have life and have it abundantly." (John 10:10)

The Christian response to a world searching for a party is not, stop pursuing pleasure. It's indulge yourself, drink until you're full, feast on the One in whom the party never ends. That's the answer that only the gospel provides. Religion says, "don't go to the party", the gospel says, "go to the party that never ends." You were created to find meaning and pleasure. As Augustine said, "...your heart will be restless until you find him." CS Lewis said, "Your problem is you've settled for mud pies because you can't even imagine what it'd be like to have a feast at the sea."

You don't get rid of idols by removing them. You destroy idols by *replacing* them.

Let me say that again.

You don't *make* a void. You *fill* a void.

Saying "I'm just going to stop. I just won't do it anymore," doesn't work. You know it doesn't work. You don't turn away from porn or the bottle. You don't stop putting the headphones of music on the heartaches of life because pleasure is bad and you just need to stop.

You do it because that sin is destroying your appetite for a greater pleasure.

Sex, wine, music, and laughter on their own fall short of the glory of God; but when your delight is in the glory of God, then you can enjoy sex, wine, music, and laughter to the glory of God. In other words, rather than these things becoming god's to which you look for meaning, they become means by which you can worship and glorify God because your delight is in Him. Then, whether you eat or drink or sing, play, make love, or whatever you do, you do all to the glory of God.

Are you settling for gluttony at the buffet when you could have a feast at God's table? Are you running to the local liquor store when you could have communion wine? Are you settling for a few jokes when you could have joy everlasting? Are you singing the same song, different verse when you could have a new song in your heart?

My fear is not that you're going to go pursue pleasure. My fear is that you're not going to pursue it enough. Don't close this book and run to the world for the superficial, or run to religion for the artificial. Both of those will miss the party in the One in whose hand are pleasures forevermore.

Chapter Twelve

"Life at the Top"

E ven though it came out in 1941, it is still considered by most movie experts, one of, if not *the* greatest movie ever made. Even today it is heralded as a masterpiece in film. The movie I'm referring to is the Orson Welles' classic, *Citizen Kane*. It's a story about a man named Charles Foster Kane. He has a very happy childhood even though his family is very poor. All of that changes when Charles receives an enormous amount of wealth, enough to enable him to achieve anything he wants in life. Charles sets out to find meaning with his money. He gains fame. He gains popularity. He gains influence. He builds an enormous estate, a mansion where people wait on him every day. He has everything you could possibly want. He has, in human terms, the good life: life at the top.

But for Charles, it isn't enough. This is shown throughout the movie by an image of a fireplace that keeps burning brighter and brighter. The desire is for more. He cannot get enough until, finally, it all comes crashing down. In one of the most famous scenes in the movie—when Charles literally self-destructs—he walks around his bedroom throwing things across the room, breaking things, turning over all the shelves. He loses it all.

Here is a man who looks at everything he's gained, everything he's accomplished, all that he's achieved in life, and he throws it all away. Why? He can't stand the emptiness inside. Then he comes across a glass globe, which he called Rosebud. He looks in the glass ball and it reminds him of his childhood. It reminds him of the happiness he no longer has. It reminds him of the peace he had as a kid. *Citizen Kane* is about a man who had everything yet he can't find peace in life.

Achievement, success, pursuing a life "at the top", may be the biggest idol of our culture. Take, for instance, all the symbols of achievement we see in our culture. We have awards and report cards and certificates. We have resumes, the list out all your accomplishments, everything that you've achieved, all the awards that you have, all the education you've obtained, all the success in your career. In many ways, you are defined by your resume.

You see, we live in a culture where we're defined by our accomplishments. What you do, what's on your resume determines who you are. Or maybe the most popular symbol of accomplishment is the trophy. Isn't everybody after the trophy? Sports trophies, music awards, movie awards? *Achievement is the alcohol of our lives.* It's addictive. When you get a little bit of it, you want more of it.

Turns out that is not a new idea; Qoheleth tried to find meaning in the same thing. He did it better than you or I could possible dream. Here is his resume: "*I made great works. I built houses and planted vineyards for myself. I made myself gardens and parks, and planted in them all kinds of fruit trees. I made myself pools from which to water the forest of growing trees.*" (2:4) He said, "houses," plural, meaning he had the beach house; the cabin up north, and the uptown apartment overlooking the city. If his life were a game of monopoly, he has hotels on Boardwalk and Park Place and owns all the Railroads. There's not a place on the board you can go that he doesn't own.

Aren't houses often a status symbol in most cultures? How big your house is, what neighborhood your home is in, how many homes or property you own? Remember, Qoheleth is a persona of Solomon. Solomon's home took 13 years to build with a construction crew of 153,000 workers. He planted vineyards, made gardens and parks full of fruit trees and pools. In fact, most scholars think this is a reference to Eden.

> "*I bought male and female slaves, and had slaves who were born in my house. I had also great possessions of herds and flocks, more than any who had been before me in Jerusalem. I also gathered for myself silver and gold and the treasure of kings and provinces.*"

He says, "I have cattle." Now, that may not seem that impressive to us, unless you live in Montana or on a ranch. Most of us don't go around bragging about our herds and livestock. In the ancient near East, cattle was a sign of wealth. Remember this is a parallel to Solomon. Do you know what Solomon's annual income was if you translated into modern dollars? It was around $800 million a year. I could live on that. Couldn't you?

He had personal servants. He has people who wait on him hand and foot. He has had servants for so long their children were born in his house. Not only that, he has trophy wives. I don't mean to offend anyone with that language, but it was literally true. Do you know how kings acquired people in the ancient near East? Through conquering lands or as gifts from other kings. Do you know why he has all these wives? Why he has all these concubines and servants? It's because he was a successful king.

He'd conquered so many lands. He has so much in his possession that he has acquired people as a result of it. He's saying, "I have everything. I have life at the top. There is not anything in terms of accomplishments that you could desire that I don't already have." You may think, "Braggart, is he just trying to show off?" Not at all.

His summation: "*So I became great and surpassed all who were before me in Jerusalem.*" In other words, "Nobody has achieved more than I have. When it comes to knowledge, nobody can touch me. When it comes to pleasure, nobody's experienced more. When it comes to accomplishment, nobody has the resume I have." He is not bragging. He is simply making the point that no one is more qualified to find meaning in these things than he is. If anyone is capable of finding meaning in knowledge, pleasure, or accomplishment, Qohelteh (the persona of a Solomon-like king) would be the perfect, and only, candidate.

Do you pursue meaning in life through your achievements? Let's run a little test, do you have servants at your home? Your kids don't count, by the way. Do you make $800 million per year? Have you conquered any lands recently? Absorbed any families under your rule and reign? I didn't think so. Me neither. So, it would be easy for us to say, " It doesn't apply to me."

Not so fast. You have more in common with Qoheleth than you realize.

Chapter Thirteen

"The Need for More"

More than we realize, we seek accomplishments and success to provide meaning in life. Let me give you 4 ways we do this.

The need for domination. Some of us, can't stand losing. Do you know anyone who is competitive? (Is it you?) What do we say in America? "Second place is the first loser." You're in second place and you're what? A Loser. Who wants the silver metal? The only thing that matters is the gold, right? We can't stand losing, whether it is in academics, or sports, or sports, or sports, or our children, or our company's success, or sports! Our identity, more than we realize, is wrapped up in winning.

One of President Trump's messages has been, "We're going to win and we're going to win so much, you're going to get tired of winning." Why do leaders say that? Because it resonates with people. Why? Because we want to win. We want to be on top. We can't stomach the idea that we wouldn't be in first place.

Do you remember the famous line in the George C. Scott film *Patton*? *"Americans love a winner and will not tolerate a loser. Americans play to win all the time. Why, I would not give a hoot in hell for a man who lost and laughed. That's why Americans have never lost and will never lose a war, because the very thought of losing is hateful to Americans."* Ours is the culture that wants to win all the time.

This is true for Christians also. It's why many Christians got upset many years ago when famous media icon, Ted Turner, said that *"Christianity was for losers."* He later apologized, but Christians got their leather-bound Bibles in a wad. They were outraged. Christianity is not for losers, after all, we have Kirk Cameron, Tim Tebow, Tony Dungy, and Mel Gibson (I think) on our side. "We are anything but losers" we exclaimed.

"Then I saw that all toil and all skill in work come from a man's envy of his neighbor." (4:4) All of us, deep down, want to be better than our neighbor. My company has to be better than your company. My church has to be bigger than your church. My resume has to be better than your resume. So often, the drive to succeed is nothing more than the desire to win. Why? Because winning is an identity. Do you know people who always have to one-up you in conversation?

"I went on a mission trip." "Yeah? I've been on five mission trips." "I had two wisdom teeth pulled." "I had seven." We don't even have seven wisdom teeth! We always feel like if I can make sure you're down here and I'm up here, then I know I matter. I have to feel like I'm a winner. We don't just desire domination, we want to be recognized, too.

The need for recognition. There are people who modestly say they don't like recognition, but all of us have had an experience where we didn't get recognized for something we felt we should have been and it bothered us. We don't get the recognition we deserve from our family. We don't get the recognition we deserve from our church. They don't recognize at our job and it hurts because recognition can give us a sense of *significance*. It strikes deeply because meaning is a fundamental need. Recognition makes us feel accepted.

The need for inclusion. We want acceptance from certain people, from a certain group. We want respect from our families, our friends, our colleagues. We want a degree from a certain school. This is what C.S. Lewis called, the fear of the outsider. We're afraid we're going to be on the outside of whatever group gives us the sense of status we long for.

Do you know the driving reason why Facebook was founded? In the movie, *Social Network*, which is about the founding of Facebook, the movie begins with, *"I needed to do something substantial to get the acceptance of the clubs at Harvard."* Why? *"Because they are exclusive and fun and lead to a better life."* Acceptance and approval form identity.

Of course, that is not only true for the creation of social media, it is also the reason for our participation in social media. We want to be included, to get likes, to have friends, to belong to some form of community. Underneath it all is a search for significance and meaning in life.

The need for a contribution. We want to make a difference. We live so that at the end of our life, we can say, "I lived a good life. I contributed to society, art, music, theology, or something. I contributed in some way."

Perhaps you are struggling with a life that never lived up to the expectations of your parents, and it has crushed you. Why? Because you've never felt like you've been good enough. If you had been good enough, if you had been a doctor like they were, if you'd had the resume like they had, if you were as successful an athlete as they were, then you would have mattered. But because you couldn't contribute, because you didn't have that skill, you were crushed under the weight of those expectations.

This is illustrated perfectly in the closing part of the movie, *Saving Private Ryan.* In the film, a soldier gets rescued by four other soldiers who lose their lives to get him home to his mother. Later on, at the end of this man's life, he visits the graves of those 4 men who gave their life for his. As an old man, he stares at the headstones. His wife and family are off in the distance. When his wife walks up to him, he turns to her and says, *"tell me I am a good man."* He wants to make sure that his life made their sacrifice worth it, that his life was enough!

Listen, you may not have the property Qoheleth had. You don't have the paradise he built. You haven't obtained a resume like his. But you, just like he was, are seeking something that will allow you to echo his words, *"I became great."* A great parent, great employee, great athlete, great pastor, great human being. There's something that your heart is clinging to so that you can say, "I've accomplished this, and therefore, I matter."

What is his conclusion? After he has pursued, and accomplished, everything you could possibly accomplish, he ends up like Charles in *Citizen Kane*. He says, *"It is vanity. It too, is meaningless."* Qoheleth realizes accomplishments never accomplish anything. Here's why.

You'll always be frustrated. *"Again, I saw vanity under the sun: One person who has no other, either son or brother, yet there is no end to all his toil, and his eyes are never satisfied with riches."* *(4:7)* The fireplace keeps burning brighter and brighter and brighter. The eyes are never satisfied. You get one trophy and you want another one. You're either get everything you hope to achieve and realize it doesn't fulfill you, or you're never achieve what your heart desperately wants.

Don't take my word for it. Listen to Tom Brady, the former quarterback for the New England Patriots. He did a 60 Minutes interview many years ago. This man has won Super Bowls, been Super Bowl MVP, been in the Pro Bowl multiple times, been Male Athlete of the Year, dated supermodels (and married one), and has made millions. He has known achievement.

Here's what he said in the interview, *"Why do I have three Super Bowl rings and still think there's something greater out there for me? I mean, maybe a lot of people would say, 'Hey, this is what is.' I reached my goal, my dream, my life. Me, I think: it's gotta be more than this. I mean this can't be what it's all cracked up to be....and what else is there for me?"* The interviewer asked, *"So what's the answer?"* and Tom Brady said, *"I wish I knew."*

Or what about Shia LaBeouf, the famous actor, from *Transformers*, *Indiana Jones*, *Fury*, and *Wall Street 2*. He said this in an interview— *"Sometimes I feel like I'm living a meaningless life. I know*

I'm one of the luckiest dudes in America right now. I have a great house. My parents don't have to work. I've got money. I'm famous, but I have no idea where this insecurity comes from because it's like a God-sized hole." Sounds like our friend Qoheleth, doesn't it?

Take it from those at the top who say you're going to be frustrated because you're either never going to be the movie star, or you're going to be the movie star and still want more. The eyes are never satisfied with riches.

You will always be fighting. Not only will you always be frustrated, but Qoheleth tells us that achievement doesn't achieve anything because the fight never ends. The striving never ends. *"Then I considered all that my hands had done and the toil I had expended in doing it, and behold, all was vanity and a striving after the wind, and there was nothing to be gained under the sun." (2:11)* So his resume, all that he'd accomplished, all the energy, all the blood, sweat, and tears that he'd put into it, was all meaningless and an unending struggle to catch…the wind.

It's a constant chase. You're going to fight to get to the top, and then you're going to fight to stay at the top because once you get to the top, you're going to say what every prisoner has said when they've come out of prison, "I am never going back there". I'm never going back to that income level. I'm never going back to that level of the organization. I'm never going back to irrelevance. So, you're going to fight all the way to get there and if you get there—maybe you will, maybe you won't—but if you get there, then you're going to have to fight to stay there. It's always a striving, like chasing the wind.

Madonna once said, *"My drive in life is from this horrible fear of being mediocre. That always pushes me because even though I've become somebody, I still have to prove that I am somebody. My struggle has never ended, and it probably never will."* Prove you're somebody, and then you're going to have to prove you're still somebody.

Qoheleth searches for meaning in accomplishments. He lays out his resume. He says, "I am great. Look at all I've done," (no bragging, just fact) but it is vanity because it only leads to constant frustration or continuous fighting.

What do you say to someone like that? Do you have an answer? The answer is, "The only place you can find meaning is in accomplishments." You read that right. Meaning is found in accomplishment. The question is, "Whose?"

Chapter Fourteen

"The Ultimate-Achiever"

W hen the Apostle Paul writes to the Philippians about the false teaching of the Judaizers, (those who taught that Gentile believers had to keep the Law of Moses to be saved), Paul addresses his own resume. As a way of showing the Judaizers that salvation does not come through personal accomplishment (living by the law), Paul makes a very impressive list of his own accomplishments. Paul says, I'm a descendant of Abraham. I've been circumcised. I've obeyed the law. In fact, *"...though I myself have reason for confidence in the flesh also. If anyone else thinks he has reason for confidence in the flesh, I have more...." (Phil 3:4)*

Paul is saying the exact same thing Qoheleth is saying, namely that when it comes to accomplishments and acheivements, no one is more qualified than he is. Paul, as a Jew, was"...*circumcised on the eighth day, of the people of Israel, of the tribe of Benjamin, a Hebrew of Hebrews; as to the law, a Pharisee; as to zeal, a persecutor of the church; as to righteousness under the law, blameless.*"

Then Paul says something that changes everything! "*But whatever gain I had, I counted as loss for the sake of Christ. Indeed, I count everything as loss because of the surpassing worth of knowing Christ Jesus, my Lord. For his sake I have suffered the loss of all things and count them as rubbish, in order that I may gain Christ and be found in him, **not having a righteousness of my own** that comes from the law, but that which comes through faith in Christ, the righteousness from God that depends on faith.*" *(3:7)* Paul's point is this, meaning is found in accomplishments, just not yours! Meaning is found in achievement, just not your own. Meaning is found in the accomplishment and achievement of Jesus Christ!

This is the beautiful doctrine of imputation, which is at the heart of the gospel. God has taken your pathetic resume and given you the resume of Jesus Christ. "*For he made him who knew no sin to be sin on our behalf that we might become the righteousness of God.*" *(2 Cor 5:21)*

The truth is, even with all the accomplishments you have gained in your life, you will never out-accomplish the cross. Therefore, you will never find meaning in life until you stop living for your resume and simply receive his resume. Then, you will be set free!

The good news of the gospel is this, Jesus has accomplished everything we need.

Earlier, I've said that when you understand that wisdom is all about Jesus, you don't stop pursuing knowledge, rather you pursue knowledge as a way of knowing God more and glorifying Him with your life. When you understand that Jesus is the party and all pleasure is about him, you don't want to stop pursuing pleasure. You want to pursue real pleasure. It is the same thing with accomplishments!

You see, the very Apostle that considered his resume "rubbish" in light of knowing Jesus more, is also the same Apostle that said, *"I labored more than them all, yet not I, the grace of God in me."* What's the point? When you're resting in the accomplishment of Christ, you're actually free to pursue accomplishment, not to be your god, but to simply worship God as a steward of all the talent he's given you.

You can run hard as an athlete and gain the trophy to the glory of God because you didn't need the trophy to be somebody. You're already somebody in Jesus. The trophy was just a part of the stewardship of speed that God gave you. You're simply taking those gifts and using them back in terms of accomplishment to the glory of God.

At the end of Citizen Kane, when Charles died and everyone has gathered around talking about his life, they say, *"Mr. Kane was a man who got everything he wanted and lost it. Rosebud was either something he couldn't get or something he lost. It was a piece in a jigsaw puzzle, a missing piece."* It's a very sad thing when people like Qoheleth, like Citizen Kane, like so many people in our culture, have everything and yet they have nothing. Jesus invites you today to stop trying to be somebody and receive the identity of Someone. He invites you to stop trying to obtain a certain life and simply receive abundant life. How do you do that? To quote that great old hymn, *"My trophies at last I lay down and exchange them today for a crown."*

Chapter Fifteen

"All You Need is Love"

Most of my childhood was spent growing up in the 1980s, which was, let's be honest, an amazing decade to grow up in. It was a decade filled with awesome contributions like denim, groundbreaking video games like Mario, break-dancing, computers, and cell phones!

Maybe the biggest contribution of all in the 1980s was the hair band. Men with enough hairspray to set the world on fire. One of the most popular "hair bands" of the 1980's was a band called Warrant. The lead singer was a man by the name of Jani Lane. Jani, like most rock stars in the 1980s, was heavily involved in the party scene: sex, drugs, and rock and roll. But he felt an emptiness inside. *Are you beginning to see a pattern?*

Jani Lane started the search for meaning in life, so he decided to quit the band in order to settle down and start a family. Maybe a family would give him significance? It didn't work. Then, he tried to give his life to fitness and joined Celebrity Fit Club. That didn't fill the void either. He was still empty, unsatisfied, and needing something else.

Finally, something happened that changed everything. He met a woman named Kimberly Nash. In an interview, Jani opened up about the significance Kimberly brought to his life. Janie said, *"No matter what I had, how many houses or cars or what I had in the bank account, or what was going on with the band or songwriting, something was always missing. Listen, I truly believe that what I needed was a soulmate. Last year, I suffered consequences from drinking that I'd never suffered before. And it made me step back and think, is this how I want it to end? The answer is no, because Kimberly makes me want to live."*

Did you read that last line? "Kimberly makes me want to live". Here's a man who has achieved music success, lived the party life, had a family and plenty of money. Yet he says, "I'm not happy. But you know what would make me happy? A soulmate. If I could just find someone to live for." He wasn't kidding. He really did live for Kimberley. How do I know? Because shortly after the two broke up, Jani Lane was found dead in a Los Angeles *Comfort Inn* with a bottle of vodka and an empty bottle of pills. When he lost her, he lost his reason to live.

What is it about love, falling in love, being in love, finding someone you can love, that gives us a sense of meaning in life? Think about all the symbols of love we have in our culture. Valentine's Day is an $18.9 billion day. Online dating estimates around 20 million people visit every month. Romance novels have over $1,000,000,000 in revenue annually. Love songs. First dates. The first kiss. Biggest of all: the wedding. Did you realize the average cost of a wedding in America is $27,000? That does not include the honeymoon. We are obsessed with love. We are obsessed with the idea of love. We truly believe love will provide meaning in life.

That is exactly what Qoheleth tries next. *"I also gathered for myself silver and gold and the treasure of kings and provinces. I got singers, both men and women, and many concubines, the delight of the sons of man." (Ecc 2:8)* Likely an allusion to Solomon, we know that Solomon had 700 wives and 300 concubines. When it comes to relationships, no one had more relationships than Solomon. He was an expert on love.

Maybe you are questioning where I am getting the idea of love. After all, the verse only states that he had concubines. Let's start by asking a few questions. First, what was a concubine in the ancient near East? A concubine was more than just a sexual servant. It was marriage-like. A concubine was marriage-like in the sense that a woman would enter into a legal relationship with the man. The man was considered to be the son-in-law of her father. Secondly, the man was legally required to provide for all of her needs. It was a legally-binding relationship.

A second important question is why would someone have so many concubines? Since Qoheleth is a parallel to King Solomon, let's ask, why did Solomon have so many concubines? Here is what 1 Kings 11 says, *"Now, King Solomon loved many foreign women...from the nations concerning which the Lord had said to the people of Israel, 'You shall not enter into marriage with them. Neither shall they with you. For surely they will turn away your heart after their gods.'"*

Notice the next phrase. *"Solomon clung to these in love."* Why did Solomon have so many women? Because he's searching for meaning and he thinks love can provide the answer. You might as well face it, he was addicted to love. He is just like Jani Lane, just like you and I, he thinks that if he can find his soulmate, then, maybe life would make sense.

Chapter Sixteen

"Two's Company, Three's a Crowd"

He was a man on the run. Hunted by his own family and deservedly so. He had, after all, cheated his father and his brother in order to obtain the birthright. By the time you get to the middle chapters of Genesis, Jacob is a fugitive, trying to escape. While his life is falling apart, Jacob encounters a man named Laben, who happens to be a relative. Laben graciously allows Jacob to work for him. As the story unfolds, there is something Jacob wants from Laben more than a job...he wants his daughter, Rachel. This became obvious one day when it came time to pay Jacob for his work.

"Then Laban said to Jacob, 'Because you are my kinsman, should you therefore serve me for nothing? Tell me, what shall your

wages be?' Now Laban had two daughters. The name of the older was Leah, and the name of the younger was Rachel. Leah's eyes were weak," [That's a polite way of saying Leah was not very attractive]. *"but Rachel was beautiful in form and appearance. Jacob loved Rachel. And he said, 'I will serve you seven years for your younger daughter, Rachel.'"*

Like Qoheleth in his search, like Solomon in his life, Jacob might as well face it, he too is addicted to love! In fact, Jacob is so in love with Rachel, he acts in irrational ways! Let me give you four examples.

First, Jacob needs food not love! Remember, Jacob is on the run, he doesn't have a job without Laben, he doesn't have anything to provide basic necessities. He doesn't have a family. He doesn't have an inheritance. He's a fugitive on the run. He needs money. But all he wants is Rachel.

Secondly, Jacob is willing to give up seven years of his life to get her. In the ancient near East, a man would normally give a father roughly 30 to 40 shekels for the right to marry his daughter. The normal wage was one or two shekels a month. So, on the high end, this should have only costs Jacob about a year and a half. Jacob is making him an outrageous and irrational offer. As the *Godfather* would say, "he is making him an offer he can't refuse." Why? Because he is in love, so much so he's willing to give up seven years to get Rachel. That's what happened.

"So Jacob served seven years for Rachel, and they seemed to him but a few days because of the love he had for her." Then, after the 7 years, it came time for Jacob to marry Rachel. *"Then Jacob said to Laban, 'Give me my wife that I may go in to her, for my time is complete.'"* He was ready

to take her as his wife. The Hebrew is strong. He is consumed with her. He wants her more than anything. She is an absolute obsession. His life has fallen apart and he's convinced Rachel will make his life meaningful.

As the story continues, Laban tricks Jacob. There's a little bit of irony here. After all, Jacob had tricked his father and brother. Now he's going to get a little taste of his own medicine. Before the wedding, Laban sends Jacob some wine and Jacob gets drunk. At the time of the wedding, he brings his daughter in full veil. She's completely covered. The wedding is performed, the two enter into the wedding chambers, and in the morning came the surprise: *"And in the morning, behold, it was Leah!"* Oh snap! Leban had dressed up Leah instead of Rachel and now Jacob is married to Leah. As you can imagine, Jacob is madder than a mosquito in a mannikin factory!

> *"And Jacob said to Laban, 'What is this you have done to me? Did I not serve with you for Rachel? Why then have you deceived me?' Laban said, 'It is not so done in our country, to give the younger before the first born. Complete the week of this one, and we will give you the other also in return for serving me another seven years.'"*

How about them, apples? Now Jacob has to serve Laben another 7 years to get Rachel. Aside from Laben's trickery and Jacobs obsession with Rachel, imagine how Leah feels. First, she's always lived under the shadow of her more attractive sister. Second, the only way a man will marry her is if her father tricks him. Third, and biggest of all, she does not have the affection of her husband. The text says,

"*He loved Rachel more than Leah.*" Sometimes addiction to love is expressed not simply through the obsession for someone (Jacob for Rachel), but also in the loneliness of having no one (Leah).

Leah is not about to give up easily. She will try her best to win the affection of her husband and she will do so through giving birth to a child. "*And Leah conceived and bore a son, and she called his name Reuben, for she said, 'Because the Lord has looked upon my affliction; for now my husband will love me.' She conceived again and bore a son, and said, 'Because the Lord has heard that I am hated, he has given me this son also.' Again she conceived and bore a son, and said, "Now this time my husband will be attached to me, because I have borne him three sons."* (29:32-34) In other words, "My life has fallen apart. This is not how I dreamed it would go, but here's how I can put it all back together, I will give my husband children in the hopes of gaining his affection.

Do you see how love is a common way people try to make sense out of life? How they find meaning? On one hand you have a man so obsessed with a woman, he gives up 14 years of his life just to get her. On the other hand, a woman who wants to be loved so badly, she will give up anything to feel the affection of a man. Love made both a slave. "I've got to have Rachel for my life to matter. If I don't have her, none of this makes sense." "I've got to have the affection of a man because that is my source of identity."

The same thing still happens today. How many people are enslaved to a relationship? How many people think beauty is their identity? Or how many spouses say, "Oh, I know what will solve our marriage problems. We'll just have children. If I have children, my husband will love me. If we have children, my wife will love me."

It's happening right now in living rooms, in homes, in relationships, all over the place. Love may top the chart of Most Popular Ways to try and Make Sense Out of Life. We see it everywhere in our culture, don't we? We see it in music. The Beatles said, *"All you need is love. That's all you NEED."* Or how about Sinatra, *"You're nobody 'til somebody loves you"*. Wow! Or even romantic icon, Willie Nelson, who said, *"You're always on my mind."* Bob Geldof wrote the following lyrics in a song called, *To Live In Love*; notice these Ecclesiastes-like lyrics:

To live in love is all there is.

Life without love is meaningless.

Life without love is life denied.

To live in love is life defined.

Life without love, absurdity.

Life without love, futility.

We see it in movies, *The Princess Bride* ("As You Wish"), *Jerry Maguire* ("You Complete Me"). *Pride & Prejudice* ("You Have Bewitched Me Body and Soul"). We have TV shows like *The Bachelor* and *The Bachelorette*. Kids movies like *Beauty and The Beast* (and pretty much all the others). We turned historical events into love stories like the *Titanic* or *Pearl Harbor*. Even sports stories like *Rocky*. (I mean, come on! Can't I just watch two guys fight without a love story!) In fact, if you took every movie that involved love away, there'd be, maybe one movie left.

The pursuit of love is found in literature. Listen to this quote from Dead Poets Society about poetry. *"We don't write poetry because it's cute. We read and write poetry because we are members of the human* race. *And the human race is filled with passion. Medicine, law, business, engineering, these are noble pursuits and necessary to life. But poetry, beauty, romance, and love, these are what we stay alive for.*"

Think about the vocabulary we use: *She's my soul mate. He worships the ground she walks on.* I'm looking for *the one*, which is really bad mathematics. We're just like Qoheleth, like Jacob and Leah, like Solomon, and our hearts are searching to find meaning and we think we can find it in someone.

This gets lived out in many different ways. There's the one who leaves his or her marriage because they're not happy. The one who thinks if I had that man, or if I could just marry her, then my life would be better. It's the couple in the clouds, planning their wedding, then six months in dealing with life on earth. It's the one who never married and feels second class. It's the one who's a single mom crying at night because her story didn't end happily ever after. It's the hookup and log on generation that doesn't understand that what they think is just sex is actually a longing and starving for significance. It's the mindset that if I'm attractive, I matter. It's the one who loses a spouse and goes beyond grieving (which is right, biblical, and appropriate), and sinks into a state of despair.

It's even the one that wants absolutely nothing to do with love. As Tim Keller writes, *"If you are so afraid of love that you cannot have it, you're just as enslaved as if you must have it."* You see, whether you're running after love or running as fast as you can away from love, the point is you're being enslaved by it. Like Qoheleth, Solomon, Jacob, and Leah, the pursuit of love is one of the primary ways people try to find meaning in life.

What do you think Quohelth concludes about love? He's been pretty consistent so far. You would likely predict him to channel his inner Adam Sandler from *Wedding Singer* and declare to everyone, "Love stinks." That's what you'd expect, but that's not quite the approach he takes. *"Enjoy life with the wife whom you love, all the days of your vain life that he has given you under the sun, because that is your portion in life and in your toil at which you toil under the sun." (Ecclesiastes 9:9)* He essentially says something nice about love, then he brings the reality check.

Qoheleth says that love is a good thing. It should be enjoyed. This makes sense as the Bible teaches that love is a gift from God. Love is something God has given you to enjoy. As we have seen on previous issues in Ecclesiastes, love is not a bad thing. Pleasure is not a bad thing. Achievement's not a bad thing. Knowledge is not a bad thing. Love is not a bad thing. God is pro-romance. He even put a romance novel in the Bible (a book Solomon actually wrote), called Song of Solomon or the Song of Songs. Let me give you a little taste of the Song of Solomon:

"Behold, you are beautiful my love. Behold, you are beautiful. Your eyes are doves behind your veil. Your hair is like a flock of goats." (Now *that* is romantic.) *"Your teeth are like a flock of shorn ewes that have come up from the washing, all of which bear twins, and not one among them has lost its young."* (Your teeth are straight, they're clean, and most importantly, you have all of them.) *"Your lips are like a scarlet thread, and your mouth is lovely. Your cheeks are like halves of a pomegranate behind your veil."* He continues to list the delights he finds in his beloved and to tell her how she has captivated his heart. Here's the

point. God is pro-romance. Love is a good thing that God has given you to enjoy.

The reality check is this: love will not provide ultimate meaning in life. He gives at least two reasons why a soulmate won't fulfill your soul.

"Then I considered all that my hands had done and the toil I had expended in doing it, and behold, all was vanity and a striving after wind." *(2:11)* That's the conclusion statement of all the things Qoheleth listed, one of which was his pursuit of love. He says, it's like striving after the wind. That idea is that idea of it's not lasting.

Love fades in feeling.

The feeling of love will come and go. C.S. Lewis (the one who lost his wife to cancer) writes, *"Being in love is a good thing, but it's not the best thing. You can't make it the basis of a whole life. Listen, no feeling can be relied on to last in its full intensity or even to last at all. If the old fairytale ending, they lived happily ever after, is taken to mean they felt for the next 50 years exactly as they felt the day before they were married, then it says what probably never was nor ever would be true and would be highly undesirable if it were. Who could bear to live in that excitement for even five years? People get from books and movies the idea that if you've married the right person, you may expect to go on being in love forever. As a result, when they find they are not, they think it proves they made a mistake and are entitled to a change. Not realizing that when they have made the change, the glamor will presently go out of the new love just as it went out of the old one."*

Here's the reality, everybody goes to bed with Rachel and wakes up with Leah. This is the reality of human relationships. It is not pessimistic at all, but realistic to life. What I mean is, every human relationship will disappoint you, even a spouse. Do you know why? Because you married somebody who's not perfect. Newsflash, neither are you. Because you're not perfect, and because they're not perfect, there'll be no such thing as a perfect relationship. Can you have a happy marriage? Absolutely. Can you be in love? Of course, you can. But if you look to that person to be the satisfaction that your soul wants, you will destroy that relationship before it ever starts.

Love also fades in the future. Qoheleth says, *"Enjoy life with the wife whom you love, all the days of your vain life."* I want to concentrate on that last phrase, all the days of your life. What's he saying? He's saying, enjoy your wife, enjoy the one that you love while you can because, eventually, they, or you, will die.

In other words, if you live for a soulmate, what is your soul going to do when your mate is gone? Death makes every love relationship temporary, and if you are looking to your love to provide meaning, when your love inevitably dies, you will end up in despair. Do you remember the story of Johnny Cash? Johnny was obsessed with June Carter. For something like a decade, he asked her to marry him. She eventually did, of course, and they had many happy years. But in 2003, June (Carter) Cash died. Johnny's diabetic condition immediately turned into a deadly one and, four months later, he died as well. I'm sure you know of couples who, after one spouse died, the other one struggled with a reason to live.

When couples die like this, we often say they died of a broken heart. Love is a good thing, but do you think it's going to bring your loved one back? Or keep them from dying in the first place? No. In that sense, love can't provide meaning in life. That's Qoheleth's point.

Is that the final word on love?

How do we respond?

Qoheleth was right to search for meaning in love. Sinatra was right, that you're nobody 'til somebody loves you. The Beatles were right. All you need is love. You've just got to be looking for it in the right Person. Let me explain.

In Romans 8:18 the Apostle Paul says, *"We live in a fallen world."* I think we can all agree with that. The world is not as it's supposed to be in. Qoheleth would completely agree. In Romans 8:20, Paul says *"Creation is subjected to futility."* Qoheleth agrees on this as well, it's vanity and like chasing the wind. In Romans 8:21, Paul points out that *"Creation is under the bondage of death."* That is, people die. And Qoheleth says, I know, that's why love can't provide meaning. Then Paul asks, *"What shall we say then?"* Qoheleth would say, "Enjoy love while you can, because it will soon end because of death."

Here's the response that Qoheleth—and we—are longing for. It's the best news in all the world. What if there was a love that death could not separate you from? If your argument is that love can't provide meaning because death makes it temporary, then what if there was a love that death couldn't end? Here is how the Apostle Paul puts it, *"He* [God] *who did not spare his own Son but gave him up for us all, how will he not also with him graciously give us all things?" "Who shall separate us from the love of Christ? Shall tribulation, or distress, or persecution, or famine, or nakedness, or danger, or sword?"* No. *"In all these things we are more than conquerors through Him who loved us. For I am sure that neither death nor life, nor angels nor rulers, nor things present nor things to come, nor powers, nor height nor depth, nor anything else in all creation, will be able to separate us from the love of God in Christ Jesus our Lord."*

Qoheleth says death makes love meaningless. The gospel says because Jesus died and rose again, there is nothing, *nothing*, **nothing** that will separate you from the love of God. Not even death. Therefore, meaning *is* found in love. But only God's love because only His love is eternal. Only His love is a love that cannot be separated by death. When your identity is the love of God, it changes everything.

When your identity is God's love, if you don't marry "the one", or when your marriage struggles, or when your spouse dies, or if you never marry...your life will not be empty because you were never looking to human love to do what only God's love can do.

This means you can actually love your spouse *more* (if you are married or when you are) because they are not your God. God is your God. The ultimate affection you need, you have found in Him, and therefore you don't have to make an idol out of your marriage. You're free to love. Why would you live for a love that will die when you could live for a love that *has* died, rose again, and *lives forever?*

Do you know how Leah got out of her slavery to love? Genesis 29:35 shows us. "She conceived again and bore a son and said, *'This time I will praise the Lord.'*" Did you see the shift? *"This time I will praise the Lord. Therefore she called his name Judah and she ceased bearing."* In other words, she found her ultimate need for affection in God. Not a man.

What came out of that? Judah. Is that significant? Absolutely! Because later on in redemptive history Jesus would come from the tribe of Judah. Jesus was the answer for Leah's search for love. He is the answer for ours as well.

If you have experienced the failure of human love, and we all have, you're invited today into a love that will never fail you. The good news of the gospel is that if your love has left you by death, or divorce, or distance, Jesus invites you to a love that will never forsake you, not even in death. The good news of the gospel is that if you're like Jani Lane, Qoheleth, Solomon, Jacob, or Leah, and you think, "If I just had a soulmate," Jesus invites you into a love that actually will make your soul complete. Until you've experienced the saving love of Jesus Christ only then will you be able to say, finally, I have found a love that's worth living for.

Chapter Seventeen

"Unsolved Mystery"

E verybody loves a good mystery. Whether it is a novel that keeps you in suspense, a movie that keeps you on the edge of your seat, or a story that keeps you wondering who "done" it. To prove this, just look at the popular shows like: *The Blacklist, Gotham, Law and Order SVU*, and *NCIS* (and its offspring), many of them are centered around solving things, figuring out mysteries, or answering clues. Of course, these current-day programs flow from a rich heritage of television mysteries, shows *Alfred Hitchcock Presents, The Twilight Zone, Murder She Wrote*, and *Perry Mason*.

The reason why these types of shows have been popular in every generation is because people love mysteries. In addition to TV shows, mystery novels are the second most popular fiction genre behind romance novels. In fact, they account for roughly $730 million in annual sales. People love the feeling of discovery when solving the problem. It's a classic "aha" moment. From Edgar Allan Poe, to Charles Dickens, to Steven King and Tom Clancy, the genre of mystery seems to be indestructible.

Of course, the most famous mystery series of all time is the legendary detective, Sherlock Holmes. The character was created by Sir Arthur Conan Doyle, a British medical doctor who created the pipe smoking detective back in 1887 for a series of short stories called, *A Study in Scarlet*. It seems like every time you turn around Doyle's fictional mystery solver pops up in yet another television show or movie. There was even one show that had the great detective living in New York and working with the NYPD.

Sherlock Holmes is a great detective for many reasons, but chiefly because of his skills at observation. You may remember one of his famous lines, *"You see, but you do not observe."* He was constantly watching his surroundings, and that helped him solve mysteries. Another key to his success was his use of science, as evidenced by another famous phrase, *"Data, data, data, I can't make bricks without clay."* He was also the master of *deductive* reasoning, using logic to try to solve a puzzle.

But there was one mystery even the great Sherlock Holmes could not solve.

It was in the television episode titled, *The Adventures of The Cardboard Box*. At the end of the story, Sherlock discovered a dead body and waxed philosophical to his long-time associate: *"What is the meaning of it, Watson? What is the object of this circle of misery? It must*

---

have a purpose or our universe has no meaning, and that is unthinkable. But what purpose? That, is humanity's great problem, to which reason so far, has no answer."

The greatest mystery solver in the world was having his own Qoheleth moment.

He looked death in the face and concluded that humanity was caught in a cycle with no rhyme or reason. Neither science or human logic seemed to be able to solve the problem. For someone like Sherlock Holmes, there is nothing more frustrating than a mystery that can't be solved.

That is exactly how Qoheleth feels at the beginning of Ecclesiastes chapter three, because he has spent two chapters trying to solve the mystery of meaning—purpose under the sun. He has asked the same questions Sherlock Holmes asked—what is the purpose? And if there's no purpose, then the universe has no meaning. It is just vanity, vanity, vanity.

It's not for a lack of looking. It's not because he hasn't tried. In fact, he has more knowledge than you could possibly have. The problem with knowledge is the more you know about most things in life, the more you wish you *didn't*. Knowledge doesn't solve the ultimate problems of life. When we looked at Daniel Tammet back in chapter seven—one of the smartest men alive today—what did he acknowledge? Logic has limits.

It's not been for a lack of having fun, Qoheleth has tried music, sex, and laughter. He has had a party unlike any party you've ever attended. The problem with that kind of party is, it keeps you coming back for more. That's the nature of *lust*. It gets you addicted and promises you things it can't deliver. It's like the great theological band, *The Black Eyed Peas*—you have to party every day. Then you have to do it again on Monday, Tuesday, Wednesday, Thursday, Friday, Saturday, and Sunday.

It keeps you coming back for more.

It's not been a lack of success. He has built houses and planted vineyards. He has an impressive resume. He has accomplished much in life, only to end up but like *Citizen Kane*. Do you remember *Rosebud*? The missing piece in the puzzle of life of John Foster Kane, a fictional character based on William Randolph Hearst, a powerful media mogul during the first half of the 20th century. Kane, like Hearst, had incredible wealth and the "toys" to show it. But when he was dying, all he said was, "Rosebud."

He was fondly remembering his sled from when he was a child.

Paul Tripp says it this way, "The problem with more is, it's never enough." That's why by the time you get to Ecclesiastes 3, Qoheleth is frustrated. He has tried everything. Yet, like Sherlock Holmes, he can't solve the mystery. So, he steps away from a personal pursuit of meaning and offers some observations about life.

What he says next is a summary of what he has observed.

Chapter Eighteen

"To Everything a Season"

H ere's a trivia question for you. What song has the distinction of reaching number one in America, according to Billboard Magazine, while having the oldest lyrics?

Hint. It was written by Pete Seeger in the late 1950s.

Still not sure? Okay, one more clue, it was recorded in 1965 by an American folk rock band called *The Byrds*.

You got it—it was *"Turn, Turn, Turn (To Everything There Is a Season)."*

This tune made the third chapter of the Book of Ecclesiastes famous.

Just because a passage is famous does not mean it is interpreted correctly. The fact is the book of Ecclesiastes is likely the most *misquoted* book in the Bible. People pluck things out, parachute in, and isolate verses without understanding the entire context. This is certainly true of this famous section of Ecclesiastes.

We've all been to funerals where this famous piece of Hebrew poetry is read.

"A time to be born, and a time to die."
"A time to plant, and a time to pluck up what is planted."
"A time to kill, and a time to heal."
"A time to break down, and a time to build up."
"A time to weep, and a time to laugh."
"A time to mourn, and a time to dance."
"A time to cast away stones, and a time to gather stones."
"A time to embrace, and a time to refrain from embracing."
"A time to gain, and a time to lose."
"A time to keep, and a time to throw away."
"A time to tear, and a time to sew."
"A time to keep silence, and a time to speak."
"A time to love, and a time to hate."
"A time of war, and a time of peace."

Not only have you heard that passage read, you've likely heard similar things said. *"There are different seasons of life. Everything happens for a reason. There is a time for life and death."*

Those statements are true, but they are not what Qoheleth means.

Go back to the beginning. When you come to chapter three, you shouldn't be surprised with what Qoheleth is saying. Why? Because the narrator in chapter one has already told you what he's going to say. Back in chapter one and verse four, he said, *"One generation passes away, and another generation comes."* That's the cycle of humanity. Groundhog Day!

Back in chapter one and beginning with verse five, it says: *"The sun rises, and the sun goes down, it hastens to the place where it rises. The wind blows toward the south and turns around to the north, the wind whirls about continually, and it comes again on its circuit. All the rivers run into the sea, yet the sea is not full. To the place from which the rivers come, there they return again."* He is talking about the cycle of creation.

In other words, what he says in chapter three is the same thing he said back in chapter 1, namely there nothing new under the sun. In other words, life is a series of appointments you can't control. Why? Because these things aren't "ifs." There will be birth and death, love and hate, embracing and refraining from embrace, planting and plucking, laughing and crying, war and peace. These are *fixed realities.* It's not a matter of *if* you will experience these things, the only issue is *when.* There's a cycle of humanity, a cycle of creation, a cycle of relationships, a cycle of war, a cycle of peace, and everyone, without exception, goes along for the ride.

Life is a series of appointments that you do not reserve and you cannot *delete.* You're stuck, like in *Groundhog Day,* in this meaningless cycle over and over and over again. You're on the treadmill. Someone has said that there are four seasons to a man's life. A time when he believes in Santa Claus, a time when he does not believe in Santa Claus. A time when he is Santa Claus, and a time when he looks like Santa Claus.

That about covers it.

I know you feel like you're in control of time. You feel that way because you have an expensive watch, or a fancy clock, a dry erase calendar on your refrigerator with all your weekly appointments, or your daily meetings all organized on your smart phone.

Yes, but, did you make the appointment of your birth? Can you delete the appointment of your death? Can you make a reservation for an emotionless life? No. You can't stop things from happening. That's the meaning of the passage. You are caught in a cycle.

How does that make Qoheleth feel? He's a little frustrated. *"What gain has a worker from his toil, I have seen the business that God has given to the children of man to be busy with translation, no matter how hard you try toil, you can't stop the cycle the business that God has given to man."* (3:9) Do you remember the famous line from William Ernest Hensley's poem *Invictus*? *"It matters not how straight the gate, how charged with punishments the scroll, I am the master of my fate, the captain of my soul?"* That's what we all want to be, the captain of our soul. Well, Qoheleth was saying in his best Matt Foley voice, "You're going to learn as you go out there, that you're the captain of jack squat."

Isn't that true?

Isn't it true when you take an honest look at life, that there are so many things in life over which you have no control? It drives you crazy, doesn't it? Being stuck on the plane in seat 23b all-the-while wishing you could be the pilot? Or better yet, in the control tower? Because you live with the assumption that if I could be in control of my life, if I could be the captain of my soul. If I could sit in the captain's chair, then maybe life would make sense. There is nothing more frustrating to Americans than the feeling that life is not in your control. It's why some of us don't like surprises. It's why some of us love rules and refuse to deviate from them. It's why everyone loves change until things change.

In my years as a pastor, there has been no theological issue that I've seen people get mad over more than the topic of *freewill*. If you want to fire somebody up, start talking about that issue because people will insist that no one, not even God, is going to tell them what to do. *I'm the captain of my soul.* I'm the one that sets my fare. I'm the one that determines my calendar.

Qoheleth says you're foolish.

You're not the captain of anything. At best you have freedom inside a captive space. You're stuck in a cycle of appointments you didn't reserve and you cannot delete. It's frustrating, not only because you're not in control, but also because you can't get all the answers.

"He has made everything beautiful in its time. Also, he has put eternity into man's heart. Yet so that he cannot find out what God has done from beginning to end." (3:11) Don't quote the first part of the verse without the second part.

There's a line from the movie, *Devil's Advocate.* The one where Al Pacino plays the devil. Here's what he says about God:

Let me give you a little inside information about God.
God likes to watch.
He's a prankster.
Think about it.
He gives man... instincts.
He gives you this extraordinary gift,

and then what does He do?

I swear, for his own amusement

...his own private, cosmic...gag reel...

...He sets the rules in opposition.

It's the goof of all time.

According to Qoheleth, God has put eternity in our hearts. We have all these questions and longings, but He won't give us any answers. It's like taking a kid to a toy store, walking him in and saying, look at all these awesome toys. There's *Pokemon* and *Ninjago* and *Mario*, all these things that you could possibly want for Christmas, but guess what? You're not getting any of it. He has the longing for something he will never get.

How will that little boy feel?

I know how my son would feel, frustrated to say the least, but angry is more likely. Why would He bring me to the store? If He was not going give me anything? Why would He put eternity in my heart, and then you not give me the answers when I need them?

He holds all the cards, and yet won't show me His hand. Or at least that is how it appears, if you are willing to be honest about life.

Life is a series of appointments that you didn't reserve and you can't delete. This means you're not in control, and you cannot get all the answers.

Verse 14 says: *"I've received that whatever God does endures forever and nothing can be added to it, nor anything taken away from it. God has done it so that people fear before him."* That phrase, *so that people fear before him*, contains the idea that God puts man in his or her place because of his *sovereignty*. God is sovereign and you can't change his plan. He has decreed it, and it doesn't matter how many people vote against it—it's happening. That leaves you helpless, if you want to be in control of life.

Charles Haddon Spurgeon, the great British 19th century preacher, is one of my favorite theologians in church history. He wrote: *"There is no attribute of God more comforting to his children than the doctrine of divine sovereignty. On the other hand, there is no doctrine more hated by worldlings."* That is, you either love the fact that God is sovereign, or you can't stand the idea. Because it means life is out of your control.

And you can't change it.

So, what does Qoheleth say? Here's his advice: *"I perceive that there's nothing better for them than to be joyful, and to do good as long as they live. Also, that everyone should what? Eat and drink and take pleasure in all his toil. This is God's gift to man."* In other words, the best that God will let you do is enjoy the life you can, while you can.

Ignore the fact that life is out of your control.

Put it out of your mind, and just enjoy what you can, because if you spend your time trying to control what you can't, if you spend your time seeking answers that God's not going to give you, if you spend your time trying to change what can't be changed, you will drive yourself crazy. Follow your mother's frequent advice: "You get what you get, and you don't throw a fit." You didn't know your mother was paraphrasing the Book of Ecclesiastes, did you? Enjoy what you can, while you can, and simply ignore the fact that you have zero control over life.

So, to summarize, just like Sherlock Holmes, Qoheleth concluded that, as unthinkable as it is, life is nothing but a cycle of times and seasons which are totally out of our control.

A series of appointments you didn't reserve and you can't delete. So, is there any hope?

Chapter Nineteen

"At the Appointed Time"

If everything in life has been "appointed," how can life have meaning? In other words, if God is sovereign, what's the point? Qoheleth feels the way so many people do—that if you were to believe in the sovereignty of God it would somehow choke the meaning out of life. But what Qoheleth doesn't see is that it's the sovereignty of God that actually gives *meaning* to life.

May I prove that to you?

How do we answer the question, if God is sovereign, then how can life have meaning? Well, first let me give you a few things Qoheleth gets right. Number one, *life is a cycle of birth and death.* People are born and people die. As much as we may want to resist this, it is reality. Number two, *God is sovereign and we're not.* He is the

Potter, we are the clay. He is Creator, we are created. Number three, *God does not give us all the answers.* Paul says *"who has known the mind of the Lord as though He needed a counselor."* Isaiah says, *"His ways are not our ways."* We simply do not have the ability to know all that God knows. So how can we find meaning in this reality?

Ponder these for a moment.

Qoheleth was right, and the reason we know this is because of what Jesus said just before He ascended to heaven following his resurrection: *"It is not for you to know the times or seasons."* Jesus reinforced what Qoheleth said centuries earlier but the part Qoheleth missed, or would not have known at the time, was that the sovereignty of God found in the gospel. Listen to the language the Bible uses regarding the most significant event in time and history, namely the crucifixion of Christ.

> *Men of Israel hear these words, Jesus of Nazareth, a man attested to you by God with mighty works and wonders and signs that God did through him in your midst. As you yourselves know, this Jesus delivered up according to the definite plan, and foreknowledge of God, you crucified and killed by the hands of lawless men. The Cross was an appointed time. God appointed a time for the crucifixion of his son.*

To further reinforce this, you may remember that Jesus, when some wanted to arrest him, said in John 7:30, that "his hour" had not yet come. There was an appointed time when Jesus was going to be crucified, but that time was not ready yet. Then, in Romans 5:6, *"You see, at just the right time, when we were still powerless, Christ died for the ungodly.*" And, one more—"*But when the set time had fully come, God sent his Son, born of a woman, born under the law.*"

Here's the point—the birth, death, and resurrection of Jesus happened at an appointed time. It was an appointment reserved on a specific date, and no one could delete it. That means that throughout the history of the Old Testament, through all the events related to the Roman government, wayward disciples, and everything in between, God had a plan. He fulfilled it perfectly, timing and all.

Why did he have an appointed time for the cross? It wasn't to frustrate us, but to forgive us. It was to solve the mystery of how we can be reconciled to God. It was to give us abundant life, not a meaningless life. Qoheleth said that appointed times mean that life has no meaning. The gospel says, an appointed time, namely, the crucifixion and resurrection of Jesus Christ is the only thing that will give your life meaning.

Wow!

Appointed times don't make life meaningless. The cross of Christ *proved* that. It occurred at an appointed time and according to the definite plan of God. It was the hour God had chosen for His son. Now, you may wonder, but how is that good news for me? How does the cross then make sense in my life? Here's how, because God appointed the cross, no matter what he has appointed in your life, you have the guarantee that it comes from the hand of a Father who loves you. The appointed cross means whatever season of life you go through, whatever difficult time you have to face, whatever season of life that's not on your calendar, know this—it all flows into your life from the hand of a Father who loves you.

The cross guarantees it.

When you're faced with a mystery, don't run to human logic. Don't run to human emotion. Tell yourself this, because God appointed the cross, no matter what I'm going through, I know it comes from a Father who loves me. That is what Qoheleth missed.

What does this mean for your life practically? First, *stop wasting time*. Because there is another day that's been appointed? It is been appointed for man to die once and after that comes judgment. This life matters and how you live matters. So quit wasting time. LIVE!

Second, *stop trying to explain life*. What you need is a big God, not all the answers. And number three, is *surrender control*. Because, news flash, you're not in control anyways. You never were. What I mean by surrender control is this: we need to learn to live with hearts of faith, not hands of control. You're never going to make sense out of life if you're living with what you can control with your hands. You're only going to make sense out of it when your heart is dominated by faith, and that's the point of Ecclesiastes—fear God and keep his commandments?

Live by faith, not by sight.

So, if there's something in your life that doesn't make sense, a mystery you can't solve a question and that doesn't seem to have any rhyme or reason at all. My advice is to surrender beneath the cross, an event in time and space that happened at the right time and according to the definite appointment of God. That's the only answer you need. Have you heard the saying, "the devil is in the details?" Well, actually, God is at work in your details. Always.

This is the only certainty you need in a life full of mystery.

Chapter Twenty

"Justice for All"

It was well after two o'clock in the morning on June 17, 1966, when two men entered a Paterson, New Jersey bar and started shooting. The bartender and one customer died almost immediately, while another victim clung to life for a few weeks before succumbing to his wounds. Two men were eventually arrested and charged with murder—one of them being an up and coming boxer named Rubin "Hurricane" Carter. They were accused of triple murder, though there was little evidence against them, they had no motive, and it was ultimately proven that some so-called witnesses had been bribed.

Hurricane Carter spent nearly two decades in prison for a crime he did not commit.

In 1985, after losing his career, his wife, his children, not to mention the most productive years of his life, he was set free. A judge dismissed all the charges, based on new evidence. He said the prosecution back in 1966 had been, "predicated on racism rather than reason, concealment rather than disclosure."

The public was, of course, outraged. Bob Dylan even wrote a song about it. It was called "The Hurricane," with lyrics that said, *"How can the life of such a man, be in the palm of some fool's hand, to see him obviously framed, couldn't help but make you feel ashamed to live in a land where justice is game?"* In 1999, there was a movie made about the story called, predictably, "The Hurricane," starring Denzel Washington as Carter.

His was a story about justice.

Of course, justice is a recurring theme and constant demand in our world. In 2020, the cries for it echo throughout the streets of most American cities, with shouts like, "No Justice; No Peace!"

It's almost as if in the minds of most people, justice equals meaning—it's what helps life make sense. When it seems like justice is mocked, people are outraged. When those we perceive as guilty (think: O.J. Simpson) go free, we are outraged. Calls for social justice are as old as our nation, from the Boston Tea Party, to the Vietnam War, to Occupy Wall Street, and Black Lives Matter.

Think about the popular superhero movies. What's the recurring theme? Justice. In fact, it's even in the name of one popular brand: "*The Justice League.*" We like to watch TV shows where the bad guys getting what's coming to them. As Christians, we speak out on issues like racism, abortion, and human trafficking. Even our children understand the basic concept of justice. How many times do they say,

"That's not fair!" It's even in the pledge to the American flag—"with liberty and justice for all." We all want justice.

So did Qoheleth.

He was trying to make sense out of a world that didn't make sense. Sound familiar? He saw three particular kinds of injustice in his day. First, there was the injustice of *consequences*. In Ecclesiastes 7:15 it says, *"In this meaningless life of mine I have seen both of these: a righteous man perishing in his righteousness, and a wicked man living long in his wickedness."* In other words, as the saying goes, "Only the good die young." When you look at the world—life "under the sun"—it is clear that consequences and outcomes are not handed out with any sense of order or—justice.

In a more "just" world, if someone ran you off the road, they would break down or get a flat tire around the next bend. If a business ripped you off, they'd go bankrupt the next week. If someone was undeservedly promoted ahead of you, they'd make a big career-ending mistake the first day on the new job. That's not how things work. People don't seem to get what they deserve.

> *I saw under the sun the race is not to the swift, nor the battle to the strong, nor bread to the wise, more riches to the intelligent, nor favor to those with knowledge, but time and chance happen to them all. For man does not know his time like fish taken in an evil net, like birds caught in a snare, so the children of man are snared at an evil time. When it suddenly falls upon them.* — Ecclesiastes 9:11-12

When I was in seminary, one of my professors and mentors shared about the struggle he and wife had with infertility: *"After I brought my wife home from the hospital, after suffering our third miscarriage, she was upstairs in the bedroom crying her eyes out. I got in the car, turned on the ignition, and the radio came on announcing Madonna was pregnant again. I stopped and said, 'Lord, here I have this godly woman who would be such a wonderful mother raising children in the nurture and admonition of the Lord. And Madonna is pregnant?'"*

It doesn't seem right, and it makes you wonder if His eye really is on the sparrow.

The next justice challenge Qoheleth saw in his day was the injustice of *inconsistency.*

> *"Though a sinner does evil a hundred times, and his days are prolonged, yet I surely know that it will be well with those who fear God, who fear before Him. But it will not be well with the wicked; nor will he prolong his days, which are as a shadow, because he does not fear before God."*— Ecclesiastes 8:12-13

If it seems like we have found a contradiction in scripture, that's exactly his point. Not only are consequences handed out unfairly, but they are handed out inconsistently. Sometimes the wicked does wrong and lives long, and sometimes the wicked does wrong and dies young. Good people get justice and good people get injustice. It's like watching a baseball game where the umpire can't decide whether a strike is a strike or a ball is a ball.

Inconsistency in sports makes us go crazy, so how much more inconsistency in life! I've seen church members go to the doctor and a random test shows cancer, but they caught it early and are eventually cured. Then, I've seen people go to the doctor for a diagnosis too late to stop the inevitable. The British pastor-author John Stott has written: *"Suffering undoubtedly constitutes the single greatest challenge to the Christian faith, and in every generation. <u>It's distribution and degree appear to be entirely random and therefore unfair.</u>"*

Qoheleth's third challenge was, the injustice of the *courts*. It says in Ecclesiastes 3:16: *"Moreover I saw under the sun: In the place of judgment, wickedness was there; and in the place of righteousness, iniquity was there."* The references "place of judgment" refers, of course, to the courts or justice system. He makes the point that the place actually set aside for justice doesn't always hand it out. Have you ever seen an image of "Lady Justice?" She is holding scales—indicating the need for balance and fairness, and she is always blindfolded, because true justice is supposed to be blind.

What do you do when, as Shakespeare said, *"fair is foul, and foul is fair"*—when the blindfold is removed, the scales are thrown out of balance, and the sword has been stolen? How often do we see stories in the media about judges accepting bribes, lawyers distorting facts, witnesses committing perjury, child molesters getting mere probation, the guilty going free, the innocent being convicted, and decisions being handed down back on political considerations and not the letter of the law? The fact of the matter is, in a fallen world there is no real justice for all.

Period.

The late Paul Harvey once told a story about a man in California who had been charged with robbery. He was in court and asked permission to visit the restroom. He was escorted there by a guard, who waited for him outside the door. Determined to escape, the man climbed up through the ceiling and into a crawl space. He crawled along for about 30 feet, when the panels broke and he fell from the ceiling—right back into the courtroom!

That's justice. That's how things ought to be!

But it doesn't always work that way. One may recall the words Henry Wadsworth Longfellow penned on Christmas Day way back in 1863, as America was being ripped asunder by a bloody Civil War. It was originally a poem called "Christmas Bells," but we know it better as the carol, "I Heard the Bells on Christmas Day." The words are haunting: "In despair, I bowed by head: 'There is no peace on earth,' I said. 'For hate is strong and mocks the song of peace on earth, good will to men.'"

Indeed.

We all want justice. We pursue it with passion. So, what are we left to do when there is no justice for all?

Chapter Twenty-One

"How Long Oh Lord?"

Qoheleth's real issue was not the fairness of life itself, or even human justice systems. No, it was the highest court of all—the throne of God. Ecclesiastes 3:17 says, *"I said in my heart, "God shall judge the righteous and the wicked, for there is a time there for every purpose and for every work."* Now, that sounds downright orthodox. God will judge. Qoheleth's theology was right!

Sometimes it's hard to apply theology to the reality of life. You know God can defeat the giants, but you are not sure he will. In fact, the Bible is filled with examples of people who struggled with the whole idea of theology vs reality. Qoheleth was no different.

Back in chapter three of Ecclesiastes we saw that life is a series of appointments we don't reserve and can't delete.

"O Lord, how long shall I cry for help, and you will not hear? Or cry to you 'Violence!' and you will not save? Why do you make me see iniquity, and why do you look at wrong? Destruction and violence are before me; strife and contention arise. So the law is paralyzed, and justice never goes forth. For the wicked surround the righteous; so justice goes forth perverted." – Habakkuk 1:1-4

Ecclesiastes 3:18-21 says:

"But the question is begged, since God is sovereign and will judge the righteous and wicked, why isn't He doing it? I said in my heart, 'Concerning the condition of the sons of men, God tests them, that they may see that they themselves are like animals.' For what happens to the sons of men also happens to animals; one thing befalls them: as one dies, so dies the other. Surely, they all have one breath; man has no advantage over animals, for all is vanity. All go to one place: all are from the dust, and all return to dust. Who knows the spirit of the sons of men, which goes upward, and the spirit of the animal, which goes down to the earth?'"

The same thing happens to man and beast—they die and who knows what their destination. C.S. Lewis wrote: *"Not many years ago when I was an atheist, if anyone asked me, 'Why do you not believe in God?' my reply would have been, 'Look at the universe we live in.' History is largely a record of crime, war, disease, and terror...if you ask me to believe this is the work of a benevolent and omnipotent spirit, I reply all the evidence points in the opposite direction."*

In other words, it was evil that actually brought Lewis to believing in the existence of God. It says in Ecclesiastes 3:22, *"So I perceived that nothing is better than that a man should rejoice in his own words, for that is his heritage. For who can bring him to see what will happen after him?"* So, go ahead and scoop that ice cream and enjoy life. It's like the musical *Fiddler on the Roof.* With the Jewish community in Russia being oppressed (injustice) by the Tsar and his secret police, the Okhrana, the main character's daughter wants to break with the traditions. There is a line: "life has a way of confusing up, blessing and bruising us, so drink—L'Chaim—to life!"

So, how do we find meaning in a world of injustice?

There must be a resolution of injustice. This is where the gospel comes in, particularly the cross of Christ. When you really think about it, the gospel offends our sense of justice. If you operate in life with the sense that people should get what they deserve, you will never understand or appreciate what Jesus did at Calvary.

"There is none righteous, no, not one; there is none who understands; there is none who seeks after God....For all have sinned and fall short of the glory of God." — Romans 3:10-11, & 23

You see, the problem with the question, "why do bad things happen to good people?" is that there are not really any good people.

We know this because of God's law. It says in Romans 3:19-20, *"Now we know that whatever the law says, it says to those who are under the law, that every mouth may be stopped, and all the world may become guilty before God. Therefore by the deeds of the law no flesh will be justified in His sight, for by the law is the knowledge of sin."*

We know this because of God's righteousness. Romans 3:21 says: *"But now the righteousness of God apart from the law is revealed, being witnessed by the Law and the Prophets."*

But how can a righteous God look at sin and do nothing? How can Abraham be a liar, and yet be designed by God to be the father of many nations? How can David murder and be a king? Isn't that injustice?

Yes, and that's why God put all of injustices on Jesus. He sent his only Son into an unjust world to be rejected by men, betrayed by friends, and falsely accused by wicked witnesses. He endured a sham of a trial and was beaten and nailed to a cross.

God, in fact, has brought us ultimate justice through the greatest act of injustice. And if can transform the ugliness of capital punishment via crucifixion into something beautiful, imagine what he can do with you and me.

Qoheleth in his day saw injustice at every turn and wondered why God did nothing about it but he didn't know the cross was coming. The gospel says God sees the injustice of the world and has done something about it.

His name is Jesus Christ!

So, what does all this mean in practical terms? It means the cross of Christ is the key to every kind of justice. It is the key to *personal justice*. The only way to find peace when you face something unjust being done to you is to live in light of the cross. In effect, you are saying: "Jesus faced more injustice that I am and he died for what is being done to me." I Peter 2:23 says, *"When he was reviled, he did not revile in return; when he suffered, he did not threaten, but continued entrusting himself to him who judges justly."*

The cross is also the key to *religious justice*. If the cross proves anything, it's that our lives are not about performance. Moral people do not always receive better circumstances because life isn't about morality; it's about God's grace.

The cross is also the key to *future justice*. The cross wasn't God's final act. We learn this from Acts 17:31, *"Because he has died a day on which he will judge the world in righteousness by a man who he has appointed; and of this he's given assurance by raising him from the dead."*

The cross is the key to *eternal justice*. The last thing we want is what we actually deserve. Qoheleth was right to search for meaning in justice, but he was wrong to search for it in this world. For as much as we hope to achieve it, the kingdoms of this world will never be able to offer liberty and justice for all. Yet, liberty and justice can be found, but only in the cross of Christ.

Chapter Twenty-Two

"The Ring of Power"

I t's one of the greatest stories ever written, with 150 million books sold, generating revenue in the billions of dollars. That's just the books. The famous film director Peter Jackson picked up the trilogy and made a movie series that has earned more than $10 billion. If you're doing the math in your head, that's a combined total of almost $20 billion that has been generated from this trilogy.

In fact, all three movies are in the top 30 movies of all time.

I'm talking about the classic trilogy written by one of the Oxford "Inklings," J.R.R. Tolkien, titled *The Lord of the Rings*. If you've watched the movies or read the books, you know the story is about a mission, a long and difficult journey to accomplish one objective: the destruction of a ring. In one of the movies, Tolkien's character, Galadriel explains:

> *It began with the forging of the Great Rings. Three were given to the Elves, immortal, wisest, and fairest of all beings; seven to the Dwarf lords, great miners and craftsmen of the mountain halls; and nine... nine rings were gifted to the race of men, who, above all else, desire power.*
>
> *For within these rings was bound the strength and will to govern each race. But they were all of them deceived, for another Ring was made. In the land of Mordor, in the fires of Mount Doom, the Dark Lord Sauron forged in secret a master Ring to control all others, and into this Ring he poured his cruelty, his malice, and his will to dominate all life. One Ring to rule them all.*

The reason the ring has to be destroyed is because with it comes great power—*"One ring to rule them all."* This is why everyone wants the ring. Wars are fought over it. Hearts are deceived by it. Relationships are challenged because of it, because everybody thinks: *"If power were in the right hands, then all would be right."*

Sound familiar?

What Tolkien so brilliantly and beautifully describes throughout the story is how power in the hands of humanity brings *vanity*. Power given to human beings can never make things ultimately right. In fact, what they do is make bigger messes.

Three thousand years before Tolkien and *The Lord of the Rings*, Qoheleth concluded the same thing.

Again I saw all the oppressions that are done under the sun. And behold, the tears of the oppressed, and they had no one to comfort them! On the side of their oppressors there was power, and there was no one to comfort them. And I thought the dead who are already dead more fortunate than the living who are still alive. But better than both is he who has not yet been and has not seen the evil deeds that are done under the sun.

Then I saw that all toil and all skill in work come from a man's envy of his neighbor. This also is vanity and a striving after wind. The fool folds his hands and eats his own flesh. Better is a handful of quietness than two hands full of toil and a striving after wind. — Ecclesiastes 4:1-6

In fact, Ecclesiastes chapter four is *The Lord of the Rings* before there ever was one. Qoheleth has been on a personal journey to find meaning in life. He tried the usual "suspects," knowledge, fun, pleasure, success, work, and love. But, his conclusion was: *temporary things cannot satisfy the eternal longings of the heart.* And he is right.

Then in chapter three, he began to make some observations about life under the sun in a fallen world. Things like: life *is a series of appointments you did not reserve and you cannot delete.* That *life under the sun is full of injustice.* Now, Qoheleth has another observation in chapter four: *Life under the sun is a constant struggle for power.*

Everywhere we look you see the fighting, striving, and battling for power. We see it in politics. We see it in relationships. We see it in marriage. We see it at work. We see it in people's struggle with authority. We even, unfortunately, see it in the church. We often assume, like in LOTR, if power were in our hands all would be right in the world.

Chapter Twenty-Three

"Power Corrupts"

T here is a constant struggle in almost any area of life for power, because more than we realize, we think, "If power were in the hands of the right people (namely, "us") life would make sense." Qoheleth concluded power in the hands of humanity is vanity. He ought to know. He had a résumé better than ours. He was a man who knew power. He was a Solomon-like king. He had tremendous wealth. He had all kinds of people following him. He had power, and he suggests five reasons why power is actually powerless to give life meaning.

1. Oppression.

"Again I saw all the oppressions that are done under the sun. And behold, the tears of the oppressed, and they had no one to comfort them!" *(4:1)* His point is that no matter who's in power, somebody else always ends up oppressed. It is usually those who oppose or disagree with the people in power.

The Hebrew word here for *oppression* means not just physical harm, though that has certainly been true, historically. It's more of a generic term. It could mean the people are oppressed by the fact that they're belittled, ignored, or taken advantage of, but the point is still the same. The weak are usually oppressed in some way by the strong.

If you don't think this is true, review your notes from history class.

This is not only true in human history, it has certainly been true in church history. For example, in the eleventh century there was a pope by the name of Gregory VII. He believed only the Catholic church had the power to appoint bishops. The King of England, Henry IV, said, "No, you don't have the power to do that. The state has the power to do that." Henry appointed his own bishop. Church and state collided over who had the power.

Henry, the king, decided to have Gregory, the pope, killed.

Gregory heard about the plot, and moved his chess piece first. Gregory announced an *interdiction*, declaring that no priest was permitted to serve communion to Henry. In Catholic theology, particularly then, if you were cut off from the Eucharist, which was God's means of grace, you were, in effect, cut off from God. Gregory's message was clear. "Henry, you may have the ability to kill me, but I can send you to hell." Needless to say, this got Henry's attention. In the middle of winter, in the year 1076, the King of England stood barefoot in the snow, begging the pope to forgive him. Gregory "had the ring" and he wanted Henry to know it. You see, whether it is husband to wife, parent to child, one race to another, government to people, or gangs to a community, oppression has been a part of life under the sun.

Power in the hands of humanity is ultimately vanity.

2. Adoration.

Oppression is not the only problem with power. Qoheleth sees another reason why power is powerless to provide meaning.

> *Better was a poor and wise youth than an old and foolish king who no longer knew how to take advice. For he went from prison to the throne, though in his own kingdom he had been born poor. I saw all the living who move about under the sun, along with that youth who was to stand in the king's place. I saw all the living who walk under the sun; They were with the second youth who stands in his place. There was no end of all the people over whom he was made king. Yet those who come afterward will not rejoice in him. Surely this also is vanity and grasping for the wind.* — Ecclesiastes 4:13-16

In these verses we see a description of how people love the person in power but that adoration doesn't last forever. *"Yet those who come later will not rejoice in him."* In other words, all the popularity you think you're going to get with power doesn't last. They will love you one day and hate you the next. They praise you one day and bury you the next. All people really want, Qoheleth is saying, is, *"What have you done for me lately?"*

Ask any pastor. Ask any politician. Ask any parent. Ask any coach. People will love you for a while. The fan base will cheer when you are winning but you're only one interception away from the doghouse, the chopping block, or the unemployment line. You're only one bad decision away from your popularity rating going down the toilet. All the adoration you think you're going to get by being in power doesn't last.

The 1970 Academy Award winning movie, *Patton*, ends with a powerful scene that is directly on point. As the great general walks on a hilltop and he says:

> *For over a thousand years Roman conquerors returning from the wars enjoyed the honor of triumph, a tumultuous parade. In the procession came trumpeters, musicians, and strange animals from conquered territories, together with carts laden with treasure and captured armaments. The conquerors rode in a triumphal chariot, the dazed prisoners walking in chains before him. Sometimes his children robed in white stood with him in the chariot or rode the trace horses. A slave stood behind the conqueror holding a golden crown and whispering in his ear a warning: that **all glory is fleeting**.*

Glory is fleeting indeed. Qoheleth has another reason why power is powerless to providing meaning in life.

3. Corruption.

"If you see in a province the oppression of the poor and the violation of justice and righteousness, do not be amazed at the matter, for the high official is watched by a higher, and there are yet higher ones over them." (5:8) In these verses, Qoheleth is describing a situation where bribes are taking place among those in power. As Lord Acton famously said: "Power tends to corrupt and absolute power corrupts absolutely. Great men are almost always bad men, even when they exercise influence and not authority; still more when you superadd the tendency of the certainty of corruption by authority."

That isn't only true in politics, it's true in business— embezzlement, tax fraud, insider trading, and many other examples. This is also true in religious organizations. In just about every arena of leadership, some version of corruption can be found.

The Protestant Reformation, for example, happened because, among many reasons, they were protesting the sale of indulgences. The priests would say something like: "When a coin in a copper bowl rings, another soul from purgatory springs." In other words, "Would you like to get your relative out of purgatory? Well, give to our building campaign."

I'm not picking on Catholicism. I am stating a historical fact, namely that the Protestant Reformation happened, at least in part, because of Martin Luther's protest of the misuse of power. In Luther's Ninety-five Theses he said, "If the pope has the power to set people free from purgatory…why don't you just do it?" (paraphrased). Why not use your power for good rather than to fill your own pockets?

Power in the hands of humanity is vanity. Qoheleth is not finished making his case as to why power is powerless to provide meaning. Another reason is...

4. Persecution.

"If the anger of the ruler rises against you, do not leave your place, for calmness will lay great offenses to rest." Ecclesiastes 10:4

Another reason power in the hands of humanity is vanity is because, people will oftentimes use power to persecute others. If the king is in a bad mood, run and hide. If dad has had too much to drink, run. If the boss is angry and he's a power-hungry boss, then freshen up the résumé.

Let me give you a Biblical answer:

Herod was angry with the people of Tyre and Sidon, and they came to him with one accord, and having persuaded Blastus, the king's chamberlain, they asked for peace..." — Acts 12:20

Why did they want peace? Because their country depended on the king's country for food. In other words, if you made Herod angry, you didn't eat. History is full of examples of this. This is often why wars are found between nations, why specific groups have been persecuted, why people have been fired from their jobs. Power is a great tool of persecution.

Power in the hands of humanity is vanity. There is one final reason why Qoheleth has come to this conclusion.

5. Folly.

"There is an evil that I have seen under the sun, as it were an error proceeding from the ruler: folly is set in many high places, and the rich sit in a low place." "I have seen slaves on horses [places of power], and princes walking on the ground like slaves."
— Ecclesiastes 10:5&7

Qoheleth's point is simple: sometimes your leader is a num-num! He or she is not bright. "I've seen folly in high places." How many of you have ever thought or even said something like, "They don't belong in that position. They're in over their head. They're not qualified. They don't have the education. They lack the wisdom."

Sometimes the people in power are those who lack the sense to use it wisely. Yet, even though power in the hands of humanity is vanity, all of us still want it.

Chapter Twenty-Four

"It's Good to be King"

It is important to remember, every person in authority is flawed, therefore, they cannot answer the quest for meaning. Qoheleth is right to be skeptical. Now, we know, based on Romans chapter 13, that government has been appointed by the Lord. Government is a good thing but when Qohelth looks at people with power, he sees ultimately vanity. Government is a good thing, but it's not an ultimate thing.

It can't make sense out of life.

It would be very easy to say, "Well, I'm not in a position of leadership. I'm not president. I'm not CEO. This doesn't really apply to me." It does. In fact, it applies to every one of us. One of the things we look to in order to make sense out of life is personal power.

Earlier, I told you that, in the Garden of Eden, Adam and Eve looked to the Tree of Knowledge of Good and Evil because they wanted knowledge. This begs the question: *Why did they want the knowledge, and why did it look so good?*

The temptation from the Serpent was, *"For God knows that when you eat of it your eyes will be opened, and you will be like God, knowing good and evil."* Why did they want the knowledge? Why did it look so good? Because they saw it as a pathway to being their own god.

Why be vice president when you can be president?

God gave them authority over the creation, but that wasn't enough and we've been eating that fruit ever since. *"If I could just have the authority to run my life, life would make sense."* Let me show you why I know that's true for us.

First, because as "king or queen" of your life, you have land or territories that are off limits to others and to God. It gets expressed this way, *"If I walk into church today and the pastor is preaching on money, preaching on a certain lifestyle or sin, I'm leaving. Why? Because that's my territory and no one is allowed into that area. I'm "god" over those areas in my life. "*

You see, kings and queens love to control their territories. That territory may be the checkbook. It may be the calendar. It may be free time. I don't know what it is for you, but I know this about me: there are areas I want to say to everybody else, *"Get out! That's mine. Trespassers will be shot!"*

Second, we have edicts or commands we expect other people to follow, and if they don't, there will be consequences. In other words,

"The right way of doing this is my way of doing this." There are relational consequences because kings and queens don't usually like traitors.

Third, and this is probably the most convicting of all—you don't like to ask for help. Are you like me, in that sometimes you tend to pray the most in crisis? Why is that? Because in crisis, we're *helpless.* The reason most people do not pray, except for in times of crisis, is prayer admits you need help and a dependent king is a contradiction in terms.

You don't pray, because prayer is what you do when you *need* a king. You need a king every day, and you're not it. That's why the Bible will say things like, "You should pray without ceasing." Every moment we need King Jesus, but if you looked honestly at your prayer life, you'd probably find more often than not you feel like you can do it all on your own.

As the late Tom Petty sang:

> *It's good to be king, if just for a while*
> *To be there in velvet, to give 'em a smile...*
> *Yeah, the world would swing [it would make sense] if I were king*
> *Can I help it if I still dream time to time?*
> *It's good to be king and have your own way,*
> *To get a feeling of peace at the end of the day.*
> *How do you get peace? When you're king at the end of the day.*
> *And when your bulldog barks and your canary sings,*
> *You're out there with winners; it's good to be king.*

We want the ring in our hands more than we are willing to admit. It is the desire to rule our own lives. We want to be king or queen, if just for awhile. The problem, however, is not power in the hands of a human, it's power in the hands of the wrong one.

Chapter Twenty-Five

"The Power to Save"

T hink about how power gets displayed in politics. People look to the kingdom of man to solve their problems. People are consumed by, angry with, and defensive about politics. If a certain party were in place or a certain policy passed, then life would make sense. People can't fathom the idea that somebody else could be a Christian and have a different political point of view.

Think of the slogans that are used in political campaigns: "Hope and Change" and "Yes, We Can" and "Make America Great Again". Why do these resonate with people? Because people want government to do for them what only Jesus can do for them, namely to give them hope and a future. People—yes, even professing Christians—seem to care little about the kingdom of God because they're involved and obsessed with the kingdom of man.

As we have learned, power in the hands of humanity is vanity.

So, what wisdom would Qoheleth's give? *"Even in your thoughts, do not curse the king, nor in your bedroom curse the rich, for a bird of the air will carry your voice, or some winged creature tell the matter."* (10:20) And… *"If the anger of the ruler rises against you, do not leave your place, for calmness will lay great offenses to rest."* (10:4) In other words—don't overreact. If you try to fight back, you're only going to make it worse.

"If you see in a province the oppression of the poor and the violation of justice and righteousness, do not be amazed…" (5:8) His advice was: *don't expect things to change.* That doesn't mean your father can't change. It doesn't mean your boss can't change. It just means life under the sun will always be this way—so get used to it. The higher your expectations, the greater the fall.

Here's Qoheleth's best advice, and it's hilarious. *"And I thought the dead who are already dead more fortunate than the living who are still alive. But better than both is he who has not yet been born and has not seen the evil deeds that are done under the sun. As much as it is within your power, don't be born."* (4:2) If you really want to avoid the absurdity of power in the hands of humanity, your best shot is never be born. Don't even come into life, because if you're born, what you're going to experience in life under the sun is that power in the hands of humanity is vanity.

As we have seen before, when it comes to this issue of power, the gospel has the ultimate answer. Do you know what that answer is? The answer is Christmas. Qoheleth was saying the kingdoms of the world cannot bring meaning, and he was right but what if there were a kingdom not of this world?

Revisit again the Christmas story.

Matthew 1:1 begins, *"The book of the genealogy of Jesus Christ, the son of David, the son of Abraham."* In other words, the New Testament starts the way the Old Testament ends—"We want a king." The Old Testament proclaimed, "A king is coming. A king is coming. There's a kingdom coming." Everybody was waiting. "When? When?"

Then the New Testament starts with the genealogy of a king.

In Matthew chapter 2, verse 1, you find, *"Now after Jesus was born in Bethlehem in the days of Herod the king, behold, wise men from the east came to Jerusalem, saying, 'Where is he who has been born king of the Jews? For we saw his star...'"* They had been waiting for a king. The word on the street is this king had been born.

Then we see how the kingdoms of the world respond when God is at work. *"When Herod the king heard this, he was troubled, and all Jerusalem with him..."* Jerusalem is troubled because if Herod is angry, you don't eat. Herod is troubled because this isn't merely the collision of church and state; this is the collision of the kingdom of God and the kingdom of man, and he's terrified. So much so that he wants this baby dead. Why? Because to his mind, it was his territory, and he wasn't going to let a little baby mess things up for him.

A bit later, in chapter 3, verse 1, we meet John the Baptist: *"In those days John the Baptist came preaching in the wilderness of Judea, 'Repent, for the kingdom of heaven is at hand.'"* His message was that the king and kingdom they'd been waiting for had arrived. Then in Matthew 4, the same Serpent in the garden and said, "Why don't you be your own king? Why don't you be a worldly king?" when he took Jesus out into the wilderness. Look at what he says in verse 8. *"Again, the devil took him to a very high mountain and showed him all the kingdoms of the world and their glory. And he said to him, 'All these I will give you, if you will fall down and worship me.'" "I'll make you king. I'll make you be your own god. You want to be a worldly king? I'll do it. Just bow down and worship me."*

Jesus did what Adam did not. He said, "No, I know who I am, and I know what I have come to do."

Chapter 4, verse 17 says, *"From that time Jesus began to preach, saying, 'Repent, for the kingdom of heaven is at hand.'"* That's the real Christmas message—"The King is here, and his kingdom has come with Him." Qoheleth said the kingdoms of the world can't bring meaning. It never was intended to, and history has proven that it will not. That's why you need a kingdom that's not of this world.

The gospel declares at Christmas there *is* a king who's not of this world, yet he came into this world, threatened the kingdoms of this world, refused to bow down to the god of this world, and He invites us to be citizens of a kingdom that's not of this world. He declared it after the resurrection when he said, *"All authority, all power in heaven and on earth has been given to me."*

Christmas is more than some little nativity set in your living room. The cross is more than a necklace around your neck. The empty tomb is more than a neat ending to a nice story. It is a declaration that a new king has come. A new regime is here, and his name is Jesus Christ.

Regardless of what a politician tells you, King Jesus the only person who can give you hope and change, who can make your life great again. He has come to do what the kingdoms of man cannot. You say, "I don't see it. When I look at the world, I don't see it." That's because you're looking in the wrong places.

If you keep reading in Matthew, you'll see things like chapter 5, verse 3: "*Blessed are the poor in spirit, for theirs is the kingdom of heaven.*" In other words, you see the kingdom, not in mighty power and strength, but in spiritual poverty. *That's* the kingdom. You see it in prayers that sound like this in Matthew 6, the Lord's Prayer: "*Your kingdom come, your will be done, on earth as it is in heaven.*" You see it when people say, "I'm no longer going to live for me; I'm going to live for him."

Do you know how *The Lord of the Rings* concludes? It isn't just with the destruction of the ring; *it's with the return of the king.* One day that will happen, not in some fictional story but in real life. The King who came at Christmas will come again in glory. Every knee will bow, and every tongue will confess that he is Lord!

Power will finally be in the hands of the right man.

Chapter Twenty-Six

"Who Wants to be a Millionaire?"

I t was just another September evening for Alex, a 70-year-old mechanic from Illinois, but his life was about to radically change. On his way home from work he stopped at the convenience store and plopped down $5 for a lotto ticket, then drove home to watch the White Sox on television. After the game, he turned on the news to hear the evening's winning lotto numbers. He jotted them down on a slip of paper and casually threw it on the coffee table. He didn't pay much attention to the numbers because his wife liked to check them when she got home.

Later in the evening, his wife returned home from playing Bingo at church. She was visibly upset because, for the second week in a row, she lost Bingo by one number. She sat down on the couch next to Alex and picked up the lottery ticket and the piece of paper with the numbers. She began to compare the numbers. The first digit was a match, the second one was a match, the third and the fourth were a match, and the fifth one was a match. This was followed by a scream of "Thank you, Jesus!" so loud the neighbors could have heard it. A week later, Alex and his wife were presented with an oversized check in the amount of $64 million.

They took the lump sum, so after taxes they pocketed $18.5 million. Alex knew his life was going to change, but he didn't know how. Honestly, all he ever wanted was to be done with the blue-collar struggle he'd known all his life. He wanted contentment, and he thought he'd now be able to find it. Instead, he developed an "out-of-nowhere appetite for more."

You see, he and his wife didn't buy a dream home, they bought eight—two for him, two for her, and one for each of their four children. One of his homes had a chapel, a basement theater with stadium seating, a 1934 *Mercedes*, a 1922 *Model T*, and several other classic antique cars. Soon, Alex discovered the newfound wealth was more burden than joy.

He was interviewed by *Chicago* magazine several years after he won the lottery. Here's what he said: "*When you do win it, you say, 'Thank you, God'—you know, you're blessed. But you're not blessed—you're cursed. Money is not happiness—it's a curse: People don't leave you alone; charities come from every direction you can think of; the government taxes the heck out of you. I don't like it.*" That's probably why he sold everything, shortly after he lost his wife due to complications from pneumonia.

After all, what good are all of those houses when they're empty?

When I read that story, I thought Alex is a lot like me. Alex is a lot like you. Alex is like so many people in our culture; those who think money will solve their problems, answer life's questions, and bring meaning in life.

In a real sense, Alex is nothing more than the product of a culture that has told us over and over and over and over again that money will make sense out of your life. We're told this from several different vantage points. The board games we play (the winner is the one who accumulates the most), or the game shows we watch on TV (*Who Wants To Be a Millionaire* or *Wheel of Fortune*), or even popular TV shows like *Shark Tank*.

It's why we have state lotteries. It's why we have casinos. The culture is constantly telling you, "Money equals meaning." Money, or course, is not a bad thing. In fact, money can be a good thing. The problem comes when money becomes an ultimate thing, and we buy into the lie that it will make sense out of life.

That is what Qoheleth addresses next in Ecclesiastes chapters 4 and 5. Before you think, "Well, who is he to tell me whether or not money can make sense out of life?" let me remind you of his résumé.

I made great works. I built houses and planted vineyards for myself. I made myself gardens and parks, and planted in them all kinds of fruit trees. I made myself pools from which to water the forest of growing trees. I bought male and female slaves... I had also great possessions of herds and flocks, more than any who had

been before me in Jerusalem. I also gathered for myself silver and
gold and the treasure of kings...(2:4)

Put all of our incomes together, and Qoheleth makes that look like a sixth grader's allowance. He was not bragging. He was not trying to make us feel bad. He was simply trying to say, "I am qualified to know whether or not money can make sense out of life." Qoheleth is not talking about whether money is good or bad. Qoheleth was not saying, "If you have money, you should feel guilty." He was simply contemplating, "Can money provide meaning? Can money ultimately satisfy you?"

He should have known whether or not that would make sense out of life because he had a lot of it. So, what does Qoheleth have to say about whether or not money can bring meaning?

Chapter Twenty-Seven

"Why Money Can't Buy Meaning"

Throughout the book of Ecclesiasties, Qoheleth highlights six reasons why money can't buy meaning.

1. The pursuit of money is often based on envy.

"Then I saw that all toil and all skill in work come from a man's envy of his neighbor. This also is vanity and a striving after wind." (4:4) For a lot of people, the pursuit of money is nothing more than the desire to either have what somebody else has, or to have *more* than what somebody else has.

They think like this: "*They* get to go on those types of vacations. *I* want to be able to go on those types of vacations." "*My* parents had that kind of lifestyle. *I* want to be able to have that kind of lifestyle." "*She* has that kind of freedom in life. *I* want to be able to have that kind of freedom in life." The problem is, even if you keep up with the Joneses, there will always be the Smiths. There's always that desire of, "I've got to keep up with them."

2. The pursuit of money won't help the lonely.

Again, I saw vanity under the sun: one person who has no other, either son or brother, yet there is no end to all his toil, and his eyes are never satisfied with riches, so that he never asks, 'For whom am I toiling and depriving myself of pleasure?' This also is vanity and an unhappy business. Two are better than one, because they have a good reward for their toil. For if they fall, one will lift up his fellow. But woe to him who is alone when he falls and has not another to lift him up! Again, if two lie together, they keep warm, but how can one keep warm alone? And though a man might prevail against one who is alone, two will withstand him—a threefold cord is not quickly broken. (4:8-9)

Often you hear these verses at weddings or as proof texts for accountability partners. However, that's not really the point of these verses. Rather, Qoheleth is saying there was a man whose eyes were set on riches, but he didn't have anybody to share them with, so he never stopped to ask, "Why am I toiling for all of this?" That's why two are better than one. His point is that *relationships are more important than money.*

Possessions are not more important than people.

There's not enough money in the world to make you feel comfortable at night, if you cuddle up next to it. It can't cure loneliness. It's what Alex was saying when he sold everything after his wife passed. "What good are all of these houses if they're empty?" Money can *never* fill the void of loneliness.

3. The pursuit of money can make you greedy.

"He who loves money will not be satisfied with money, nor he who loves wealth with his income; this also is vanity. When goods increase, they increase who eat them, and what advantage has their owner but to see them with his eyes?" (5:10) When the goods increase, the consumers increase. That is wisdom literature's way of saying, when your income goes up, so do your expenses. If you're greedy with a little, you will be greedy with a lot.

Alex is the perfect example. He thought he'd be content once he hit the lottery. Instead, what he got was an out-of-nowhere appetite for more. Winning the lottery didn't solve the issue in his heart. *ESPN* did a fascinating documentary called *Broke*. They documented that 60 percent of NBA players and 78 percent of NFL players, within two years of retiring from the game, are either bankrupt or under so much financial stress it ruins their life.

They said the competitive nature that carried them to victory on the field brought them to ruins off the field. Money is never going to solve the greed issue. If you want more now, you'll want more then. That's the point.

Alex said when news got out that he won the lottery, he got letters from strangers and relatives he didn't even know. Even his best friends said, "If you want me to still be your friend, I want cash gifts every year." Qoheleth is exactly right, when goods increase, so do those who eat them. Money can't provide meaning, because it won't solve that problem of greed.

4. The pursuit of money can bring more anxiety.

"Sweet is the sleep of a laborer, whether he eats little or much, but the full stomach of the rich will not let him sleep." (5:12) Money will solve certain anxieties, but it's also going to create others. You tend to either be worried that you'll get enough or worried that you will lose what you have.

A couple of years ago, there was a famous *Travelers Insurance* commercial about a dog constantly dreaming of a bone he wanted. It's all he thought about. He finally got the bone, and then he became worried that some other dog was going to take the bone, so he hid it under the rug. He thought, "It'll be safe there." But he was still worried about it. "What if somebody finds it?" So, he went out and buried it in the backyard.

Then he thought, "But what if somebody finds it there?" so he dug it back up and took it to the bank and put it in a safety deposit box. He thought, "Oh, but what if somebody finds it there?" so he bought an insurance policy so he knows it'll be safe. As though insurance will guarantee it. The idea there is the one thing he wanted he finally got, and then he was constantly worried about it. "Will it be taken away?"

Proverbs 23:4 tells us, *"Do not weary yourself to gain wealth..."* If you have it, fine, but don't weary, don't be anxious for it. *"...cease from your consideration of it. When you set your eyes on it, it is gone. For wealth certainly makes itself wings like an eagle that flies toward the heavens."* Money is not a bad thing, but it won't solve your anxieties. It will just create different ones.

5. The pursuit of money won't prevent tragedy.

"There is a grievous evil that I have seen under the sun: riches were kept by their owner to his heart and those riches were lost in a bad venture. And he is father of a son, but he has nothing in his hand."(5:13) Qoheleth was telling us that there was a guy so protective of everything that he hoards it. Everything is secure, and then for some reason, it's gone. All the money he had couldn't stop the tragedy from happening. Can you think of something that could happen in life that could make money go away? Stock market crash, theft, a disease where you would need ongoing treatment that sucks all the money out of your savings. The point is all the money in the world can't prevent tragedy, much less a tragedy that may take that money away.

Just ask an Israeli woman, a daughter who decided she would buy her mom a new mattress. She wanted to surprise her mom by having the mattress delivered and the old one thrown out. What the daughter didn't realize was that her mom had been storing away money over years and years and years, and when she threw away the old mattress, she threw away almost one million dollars. Who puts a million dollars in their mattress? Regardless, the point is that even in the safest place she knew, her money wasn't safe.

6. The pursuit of money won't keep you from mortality.

"As he came from his mother's womb he shall go again, naked as he came, and shall take nothing for his toil that he may carry away in his hand. This also is a grievous evil: just as he came, so shall he go, and what gain is there to him who toils for the wind?" (5:15)

Whether you want to hear it or not, you were born penniless, and you're going to die penniless. As you came, so shall you go, and there's not enough money in the world to keep that day from coming. All the money in the world won't prevent death. You don't need to take Qoheleth's word for it, just listen to the man in black...

Chapter Twenty-Eight

"Empire of Dirt"

If you don't want to take Qoheleth's word for it, listen to one of the greatest musicians who has ever lived, Johnny Cash, who looked back over his history-making life in country music and called it an empire of dirt. It's not that it was bad. It just didn't fulfill him. The problem is most of us don't think this applies to us. I've never had somebody come to me and say, "Pastor, would you pray for me? I'm struggling with a sin. I'm struggling with *greed.*"

Nobody has ever said, "Pastor, pray for me. I spent so much money on myself recently. I just feel bad about it." Nobody has ever done that. Why? Because we don't think this is our problem. The problem with greed is it's very sneaky. It can come into your life in such a way that you don't even notice it. We start daydreaming about it. We're always thinking about more ways to make it. We have a list of desired possessions. Shopping becomes therapeutic. As the country music song says, "Money can buy you a boat and a truck to pull it."

It's not just money; it's what money provides. Before long, it slips in, and we begin to love that thing rather than the one who provided the thing. We love the gift rather than the Giver of that gift. Or we trust it more than we trust God. For instance, on our currency, the phrase, "In God We Trust" is probably our culture's biggest irony. Our culture doesn't trust in God. Our culture trusts in money. If we wanted to be accurate, we'd write on the dollar bill "In *this* we trust." We call financial instruments *securities*. I feel secure not in my heavenly Father. I feel secure in what I have.

It begins to affect your behaviors and your decisions. You're worried about it. Relationships are impacted based on money. You choose a job based on salary and not family. You fall for a "get rich quick" scheme. You're angry over an issue of inheritance. Your emotions and decisions become impacted over *that*, and that's a sign that you are serving it rather than it serving you to the glory of God.

Listen to what the Apostle Paul said in 1 Corinthians 6:9: *"Or do you not know that the unrighteous will not inherit the kingdom of God? The sexually immoral, idolaters, adulterers, men who practice homosexuality, thieves, nor the **greedy**, drunkards, revilers, swindlers will inherit the kingdom of God."* The Word of God says the greedy won't inherit the kingdom of God because they're not living for the kingdom of God.

We need to be careful not to dismiss what Qoheleth was saying, because it could be that we're looking to money to be our provider of meaning more than we realize. Here's what he would say you should do with your money, in case you're curious. *"Behold, what I have seen to be good and fitting is to eat and drink and find enjoyment in all the toil with which one toils under the sun the few days of his life that God has given him, for this is his lot. Everyone also to whom God has given wealth and possessions and power to enjoy them, and to accept his lot and rejoice in his toil—this is the gift of God." (5:18)*

In other words, "The best you can do is enjoy your money while you can, because there's no guarantee God will let you keep it tomorrow." There are no guarantees. Money can't keep you from tragedy. What if tragedy happens tomorrow and you lose it all? So, the best you can do is enjoy today. Enjoy now. That's the best you can do, according to Qoheleth.

Aren't you glad the gospel gives us a better answer than that?

Look at Luke 12:13. *"Someone in the crowd said to [Jesus], 'Teacher, tell my brother to divide the inheritance with me.' But he said to him, 'Man, who made me a judge or arbitrator over you?' And he said to them, 'Take care, and be on your guard against all covetousness, for one's life does not consist in the abundance of his possessions.'"* Here was a man who put money over relationships. Sound familiar?

Ecclesiastes says, "Two are better than one."

Jesus discerned his heart, and he gave him the conclusion Ecclesiastes gives—"Money can't provide meaning. Your life isn't the sum total of what you have. Possessions are not going to give you what your heart really wants. In fact, let me tell you a story about it."

"And he told them a parable, saying, 'The land of a rich man produced plentifully and he thought to himself, 'What shall I do,

for I have nowhere to store my crops?' And he said, 'I will do this: I will tear down my barns and build larger ones, and there I will store all my grain and my goods. And I will say to my soul, 'Soul, you have ample goods laid up for many years; relax, eat, drink, be merry.''

Where have we heard that before?

In other words, you have somebody with the wrong provider. His security is in his stuff. He has the wrong perspective. He's only thinking about how he can enjoy all of his stuff right now. His perspective is, "I have a few years, but I'm not worried about beyond that. I'll just enjoy all that I have been given, and I will eat, drink, and be merry." That's an exact quote from Ecclesiastes.

Now comes the shocker. *"But God said to him, 'Fool! This night your soul is required of you, and the things you have prepared, whose will they be?'"*

Qoheleth told you there's not enough money in the world, there are not enough barns filled with grain in the world to keep tragedy from happening. There's not enough money in the world to keep you from death. You see, Jesus said the same thing as Qoheleth, but then he gave an application that was radically different, and it is the only way you will find meaning. Not only that, it will make you incredibly rich.

Chapter Twenty-Nine

"Rich in God"

What if there was a different economy? What if there was a different currency? What if there was a different security you could have rather than barns filled with grain? What if rather than being rich in *this* world you could be rich in another? In other words, Qoheleth was saying, "Money can't bring meaning, so live for the now." Jesus was saying, "Money can't bring meaning, so live now for eternity." Lay up treasures in heaven. Be rich in God. That's how you find meaning. Do you know why? Because that currency won't end. That economy won't collapse. That money will never be taken away, because it's not a possession; it's a person who lives forever.

You might say, "But if I were to surrender myself to that, how would I feel secure tomorrow?" *"Fear not, little flock, for it is your*

Father's good pleasure to give you the kingdom." That's security. Instead of living for a stock market that's up one day and down the next, what if you found your security in Jesus who is the same yesterday, today, and forever? What if instead of finding a guarantee that you are taken care of in cash, you found that guarantee in a *cross?*

What if the cross was a guarantee that you have a heavenly Father who will take care of you far much more than any other person, any other institution in this world? *Fear not, little flock.* What are you afraid of? What are you anxious about? It is your Father's good pleasure to give you a kingdom. That and that alone is the only way you will find meaning.

Let me share five things to think about relating to your life and possessions.

1. Make God your treasure.

More than anything else, God must be your treasure. In fact, this is what it means to be a Christian, that you want God more than anything else in life. A Christian treasures God—*ultimately.*

2. Make generosity a practice.

You're looking for daily, weekly, big and small ways to be a blessing. A lack of generosity is a sign of slavery. You're not willing to bless others because you want to keep it all for yourself. If you're going to be tapped into kingdom thinking, generosity has to be a part of your practice.

3. Make gospel goals with your money.

Just as you plan for a vacation, just as you plan for how much you want to save this year, you also need to sit down and think, "What type of gospel impact do I want to make? What young people do I want to invest in? What missionary work do I want to invest in? How do I want to channel what God has given me for the kingdom of God, not the kingdom of self?"

4. Make gratitude a part of daily worship.

Do you know what the gospel of grace means for us? God doesn't owe us a dime. We don't even deserve to live, much less have anything in life. What's the essence of grace? He has given you what you do not deserve. So, you wake up every day going, "This is amazing! I have a bed, and there's a car in the driveway, and a home. God is good!"

You have to live with that kind of amazement and wonder and awe at God's grace. Otherwise, you're going to be in bondage to what you have. But when you realize it's totally a gift of worship to God to say, "Thank you for what you've given me." Whether that's a lot or a little in your estimation, it's still a gift of grace.

Entitlement is the enemy of grace.

5. Enjoy the gifts God has given you.

Enjoy your vacations. Enjoy your vehicles. Enjoy your home, whatever it is you have. The Bible never tries to make anybody feel guilty for having things. Enjoy those as the gifts of God *only if* he is your treasure, generosity is your practice, you have gospel goals, and you are daily grateful for what God has given you. When those things are in place, then be grateful for whatever God has given you, you can sit back and say, "I will eat and drink to the glory of God."

I want you to be rich in God by finding the treasure of your heart in God, because that is a treasure that will not grow old, a treasure that will never fade. When you understand all that God has done for you in the person of Jesus Christ, you will not need, like Alex, to go buy a lotto ticket, because you've already hit the jackpot.

Chapter Thirty

"Searching for Meaning in the House of God"

I still remember the day it happened, and I remember where I was. My guess is many of you do too. I had just arrived at my office when I was notified by my assistant, "You need to get down here quickly." I rushed down the hall and walked into the front office. I remember specifically looking at the TV at those images that are forever in our minds—the attacks of 9/11. How many of you remember where you were on that day? My guess is not only do you remember it, you may also remember, shortly after, people flocked to church. Churches were crowded.

Wall to wall attendance.

Most churches saw anywhere from 25 to 50 percent increase in attendance. Ed Young, who's a pastor of a large church in Texas, was interviewed and said, "After 9/11, we had over 20,000 people in attendance. It was the largest crowd in our history." You may also remember those numbers didn't last long. Young went on to say, "I was disappointed the next weekend when we dropped to 16,000 and then 14,000 the weekend after that."

The rapid decline was well documented in the media. *USA Today* had an article titled, *Quick Dose of 9/11 Religion Soothes but Doesn't Change.* *Fox News* had a headline, *Church Attendance Back to Normal.* Another media outlet said, *A Short-Lived Rush to Church.* George Barna of the *Barna Research Group* said something fascinating: "After the attack, millions of nominally churched or generally irreligious Americans were desperately seeking something that would restore stability and a sense of meaning to life."

They sought meaning...in the house of God.

In other words, a horrible event happened, and that event caused people to start saying, "Wait a minute. This doesn't make any sense. I've got a lot of questions. I need answers." Instead of looking to things like work or pleasure or money, they looked to *spirituality* to give them meaning in life.

That is not only true for national tragedies, it's also true for personal ones—the loss of a spouse, the loss of a job, a bad medical report, or an economic crisis in your life. It may not be work that you turn to, it may be church or prayer or religion. Qoheleth, the wise man in Ecclesiastes, had seen it a thousand times. He had seen the aftermath of 9/11 before there was a 9/11. It happened all throughout the ancient near East, particularly in the life of ancient Israel.

"Help, God! The Egyptians are coming. Don't you see they're about to kill us? All we see is water." God splits the sea, and they make it out alive. What happens next? "Look at those golden calves. Let's worship them."

"Assyria is coming. God, help! This doesn't make any sense. Give us some answers! Oh, look at the god Ashur. Maybe we should worship him."

"We're hungry! Feed us! You've promised us a land of abundance flowing with milk and honey. Those giants are awfully big."

He has seen it a thousand times, and this wise man is giving you his observations about life, whether you want them or not. One of his observations, as he looks at the landscape of religion in the ancient near East, is this: "I see a lot of people running to God for answers in life with no intention of making him Lord of their life."

People run to spirituality with no sense of really desiring God. It's like what we see in John 6. "We don't want Bread of Life; we just our stomachs full again, and if we're hungry again tomorrow, we'll come back and find you, Jesus." Oh, 9/11 wasn't new under the sun in regard to the spiritual landscape of people wanting to worship in the midst of a crisis.

To that, Qoheleth gives a warning. *"Guard your steps when you go to the house of God." (5:1)* Translation: Be cautious. Be on guard. *"Be not rash with your mouth, nor let your heart be hasty…". (5:2)* What he's saying is "Proceed with caution when you go to worship. You want to go to the temple? You want to go worship? You might want to rethink that."

Now why would he say worship is so risky? Probably because of things like this. Leviticus 10:1: *"Now Nadab and Abihu, the sons of Aaron, each took his censer and put fire in it and laid incense on it and offered unauthorized fire before the Lord, which he had not commanded them. And fire came out from before the Lord and consumed them, and they died..."*

That might get your attention.

You don't walk into the temple in the Old Testament, grab your latte, and play church for an hour unless you have a good life insurance policy. You might say, "Thank goodness we don't live in the Old Testament. We live in the New Testament." All right. In 1 Corinthians, chapter 11, where they were messing around with the Lord's Supper. Paul says: *"Let a person examine himself, and so eat of the bread and drink of the cup. For anyone who eats and drinks without discerning the body eats and drinks judgment on himself. That is why many of you are weak and ill, and some have died."* Or what about Hebrews 12:28? *"Therefore let us be grateful for receiving a kingdom that cannot be shaken, and thus let us offer to God acceptable worship, with reverence and awe, for our God is a consuming fire."*

God is a holy God. He is so incredibly holy that even angelic beings say to God every day, all day, "Holy, Holy, Holy is the Lord God Almighty!" There are no gods before him. No nation can rise against him. No power can overthrow him. He is not to be belittled, played with, downsized, or mocked. He is, always has been, and always will be a consuming fire.

That's who you're dealing with when you come into the presence of the Lord.

That reality will do one of two things. It will create in you a healthy approach to worship (reverence and awe) or it will create in you an unhealthy approach to worship (distance and disconnect). You start to feel like God is out to get you, so you're guarded.

There is an old *Far Side* comic strip called "God at His Computer." There is a guy walking down the street, and he doesn't know there's a piano over his head. You scale back, and there's God, who is an old man with white hair, about to hit a button on his keyboard. The button says "Smite." In other words, God at his computer is just waiting to drop the piano on his head.

My guess is some of you may think that way about God, because when something bad happens in your life, your first thought is, "God, why are you punishing me?" as though God is in heaven with a baseball bat waiting to hurt you.

You step one inch out of line, and whammy. Honestly, I have felt this way before...

Chapter Thirty-One

"Promises, Promises"

O nce, when I was playing basketball in high school, I got elbowed in the nose. The pain was unbelievable. Blood was everywhere, and my first thought was, "God, what did I do wrong? What are you getting back at me for?" That unhealthy view of God begins to create in us a desire for distance.

"For when dreams increase and words grow many, there is vanity; but God is the one you must fear." (5:7) He was not talking about fear of the Lord in the healthy sense. He's talking about fear of the Lord in the unhealthy sense. We know this from the context of the passage, and the context of the entire book.

Qoheleth was advocating distance from God because you may get yourself in trouble. The reason worship is so risky is because the tendency for most of us is to go through a routine. That's dangerous. *"Guard your steps when you go to the house of God. To draw near to listen is better than to offer the sacrifice of fools..."*

Note the comparison. There are some people who draw near to listen, and there are some people who are just offering the sacrifice of fools. They're just going through the motions. Qoheleth was saying, "When I look at spirituality in the ancient near East and people going to the house of God, most of it is routine and pointless."

It was no different than a weekly trip to Walmart. It's what they've done all their life. They were just hanging out with friends. They sing some songs, hear a message, give a little bit of money, recite a creed, do a sacrament, then leave, not any different whatsoever.

Qoheleth would say, "That's insane! Given how high the stakes are...you're going to play church. You're really going to play temple?" He's just saying what God already said. Here's what God says of his own people and their worship. Isaiah 1:12: *"When you come to appear before me, who has required of you this trampling of my courts? Bring no more vain offerings; incense is an abomination to me. New moon and Sabbath and the calling of convocations—I cannot endure iniquity and solemn assembly. Your new moons and your appointed feasts my soul hates; they have become a burden to me; I am weary of bearing them. When you spread out your hands, I will hide my eyes from you; even though you make many prayers, I will not listen; your hands are full of blood."*

Translation: Do you want to know what God hates? God hates this: when worship is only external action with no change of heart. "Raise your hands all you want. Pray. Sing. Sing so loud you get goose bumps. I don't even hear a word, because it's just the machine of worship." Qoheleth saw this happening, at least in the ancient near East, in two primary ways.

The first one is *wordy prayers*, people who try to impress God with their impressive prayers. There's no heart engaged, whatsoever. Qoheleth says, "Don't be rash with your mouth..." Your prayers. "...nor let your heart be hasty to utter a word..." You go on and on and on and on. "...for God is in heaven and you are on earth."

Why is this a problem? Because the focus of that kind of praying isn't God. It's *us*. "Did I use the right words? Did I look good? Did people like what I said?" By the way, sometimes people won't pray publicly for the same reasons. In other words, "I'm not going to pray because I don't want to look bad. I might use the wrong words." What's the root of that? The core of that is "I want to look good, not worship God."

We just ramble on and on. The famous 19th century evangelist, D.L. Moody, said, "Some of our prayers should be cut short on both ends and set on fire in the middle." If you're feeling like I'm pushing the line, it's what Jesus said in Matthew 6:5: *"When you pray, you must not be like the hypocrites. For they love to stand and pray in the synagogues and at the street corners, that they may be seen by others. Truly, I say to you, they have received their reward."*

The problem is not praying in public. The problem is praying for publicity. It's praying the routine prayer so you can mark it off your checklist. In Luke chapter 18, Jesus told the story of the Pharisee and the tax collector. You have one guy. He's in the temple. He's dressed right. He probably has on a suit and tie. He looks good. He has the right posture. He says the right words. "I'm not like *this*. I'm not like *that.* I'm not like *this.* I'm not like *that.* I do *this* and I do *that."* He is so incredibly impressive. If you were in the temple that day, you'd look at that guy and say, "Man, he'd make a good elder. Sign that guy up." Then over in the corner we have an outsider. He doesn't even hold his head up. He's not even saying the right words. He doesn't even know what to say.

His prayers are so tiny. They're so small. It's only one sentence. All he said was, "God, have mercy on me, a sinner." One sentence. That's it. Yet, Jesus says, *"That man went home justified."* God wants real prayers, if if they are one sentence and you stutter your way through.

It's not just wordy prayers that Qoheleth sees, it's also *weak promises.* Verse 4: *"When you vow a vow to God, do not delay paying it, for he has no pleasure in fools. Pay what you vow. It is better that you should not vow than that you should vow and not pay. Let not your mouth lead you into sin, and do not say before the messenger that it was a mistake. Why should God be angry at your voice and destroy the work of your hands?"*

In other words, he was saying, " Not only do people pray prayers they don't mean; they make promises they have no intention of keeping. They vow vows, and they have no intention whatsoever of keeping those vows."

How many of you have ever said, "God, if you get me out of this, I promise I will...give a little, go to church, become a monk," or whatever. You said, "God, I make a vow." You didn't give any thought to it. You just wanted out. "I promise I'll do this."

Qoheleth said, "Don't do that."

Not only *those* kinds of vows, but what about other vows you made before the Lord? Marriage vows? Membership commitments? Baby dedications? Did you intend to take those things seriously? If not, you are playing with fire. Look at verse 6 again, the last phrase. He said, *"Why should God be angry at your voice and destroy the work of your hands?"* Qoheleth was saying, "Don't make him angry, because what he may do is destroy the work of your hands." The best you can do is eat, drink, and be merry because tomorrow you're going to die. The work of your hands is all you can enjoy while you can.

He was essentially saying, "Since there are no guarantees in life anyway, the odds are going to go down significantly if you poke God with a short stick of your empty promises." *"Therefore let your words be few."* Say as little as possible, because you may get yourself in trouble. Worship is risky, because most of the time it's routine with your praying and promises, so the best you can do is zip it.

Has your mouth ever gotten you in trouble? A lot of us know what it's like to have experienced that moment where we thought, "I wish I would have just kept my mouth shut. I wish I would have just been quiet." Like, husbands, sometimes it's best to not say a word. It's not going to help. Or some of you have those children who have to get the last word in. Or politicians who could use a little less time on *Twitter.* Or what Qoheleth would say is "Worshipers who should pause before they promise." Don't let your mouth write checks your lifestyle can't cash. What, are you crazy? God could smite you.

"So, here's my advice," Qoheleth would say. "The best you can do, given what's at stake, is say as little as possible. Appease God with your worship, but don't get yourself in trouble." Qoheleth's summary was "Worship is risky because it tends to be routine and God doesn't like routine, so be reserved." He's right in this sense. God *is* holy and worship *should* be taken seriously. You shouldn't come to God with wrong motives, with half-hearted prayers or promises you don't mean.

Jesus turns everything Qoheleth has said on its head. First John 4:10 says, *"In this is love, not that we have loved God but that he loved us and sent his Son to be the propitiation for our sins."* That word *propitiation* simply means sacrifice, or "that which satisfies." Translation: God loves you so much he sent Jesus to be your sacrifice. That changes everything about our worship. Let me show you how.

Chapter Thirty-Two

"Real Worship"

"By this is love perfected with us, so that we may have confidence for the day of judgment [to stand before God], because as he is so also are we in this world. There is no fear in love, but perfect love casts out fear. For fear has to do with punishment, and whoever fears has not been perfected in love." —I John 4:17

1. Because of Jesus, you don't have to be afraid to approach God.

We have something now that Qoheleth didn't know back in the Old Testament. They were looking for it, but it hadn't happened yet. The Cross. The good news of the gospel is that God has hit the "smite" button. It's called *Calvary*.

That's why we can come and worship and not walk on eggshells and not be afraid, it's why we can laugh and enjoy and be serious all at the same time, the worship of God, when we come genuinely in the name of Christ. Do you want to avoid worship that is risky? There's only one way. You have to come in Jesus' name.

2. Because of Jesus, worship should not be routine.

Remember in John 4 when Jesus encountered the Samaritan woman? He told her about her past—all her husbands, all her background, and all of her relationships. She responded, "You're probably a prophet, a religious man. Let's talk about worship. You know what? Our fathers say you're supposed to worship at *that* mountain. I know you Jews say it's in Jerusalem, but..."

What was her paradigm? Ritual. Routine. "You go to this mountain, and then you pray that prayer, and you do that thing. I know some of you do it in Jerusalem, and that's fine. The thing is you just do that. That's what worship is." Then Jesus dropped the bomb that changed the worship paradigm forever.

> *"But the hour is coming, and is now here, when the true worshipers will worship the Father in spirit and truth, for the Father is seeking such people to worship him. God is spirit, and those who worship him must worship in spirit and truth.' The woman said to him, 'I know that Messiah is coming (he who is called Christ). When he comes, he will tell us all things.' Jesus said to her, 'I who speak to you am he.'"* — John 4:23

What did he just say? "It's not ritual anymore. It's not routine anymore. It's relational, because it's not about a mountain; it's about a person." Get your mind off rituals and get it on the risen Christ, because if you don't, you're not worshipping. I don't care what elements of worship you have. Worship isn't about elements; worship is about Messiah, which means the question is not "Did you like the worship?" It's this: "Did you encounter Christ?" Anything short of that is meaningless and dangerous. Yet many Christians in many churches will go on talking about what mountain it's supposed to be on, and they'll miss worshiping in spirit and truth the person of Jesus Christ.

Do you want to avoid routine worship? Here's how you do it. You focus on Jesus, not your preference, and you encounter the living Christ.

3. Because of Jesus, worship does not need to be reserved.

Should you play it safe in worship? In the book of Hebrews, the writer is writing to some Christians who were considering playing it safe. If they go back into Jerusalem, it's safe. If they keep pressing on with Jesus, they're going to be persecuted. So, the writer of Hebrews says this in chapter 10, verse 19.

> *"Therefore, brothers, since we have confidence to enter the holy places by the blood of Jesus by the new and living way that he opened for us through the curtain, that is, through his flesh, and since we have a great priest over the house of God, let us draw near with a true heart in full assurance of faith, with our hearts*

sprinkled clean from an evil conscience and our bodies washed
with pure water."

What's the point? Qoheleth was saying, " Why would you draw near? Do you realize the stakes? Do you realize the consequences?" The writer of Hebrews asks a completely different question. "How could you *not* draw near?" The curtain is torn. Why wouldn't you come and access God when Christ has provided that opportunity for worship?

It's really sad to think about the many people after 9/11 who ran to church for meaning but didn't find it. They got temporary comfort, but they didn't get Christ. What may be even more sad than that are the people who sit in church every single week and don't experience Christ. They have a really good routine, but they've never experienced the real thing.

Qoheleth's advice is "Play it safe; keep your distance," but the gospel calls to you this: Look to the one who tore the veil and don't be distant. Draw near. Because of Jesus Christ, we don't have to guard our steps.

We can fully engage our hearts.

Chapter Thirty-Three

"No Satisfaction"

H e's one of the most popular personalities on radio. He started his radio career in 1985 and has been named the national syndicated personality eight years in a row. He has interviewed superstars, celebrities, Hollywood personalities, and everybody in between. He is also the highest paid radio personality, thanks to a $400 million contract he signed with *SiriusXM* radio. That equates to $2,000 every minute he's on the air.

Can you imagine?

I'm referring to Howard Stern. If you do not know who Howard Stern is, my advice is to *keep it that way*! While Howard Stern is certainly not an example to follow in life, he is an example of where a lot of people are in life. He did an interview with *Rolling Stone* magazine right after he signed that big contract. They talked about his career and success. One of the things he said was that was fascinating, was, "*I enjoy doing the radio show every day, but the attention I devote to it and the inability to get rid of the insecurity is very fatiguing. The curse is I take it so seriously. I can't walk out and say, 'I did a good show. I'm satisfied.' That's the source of all the problems for me.*"

This from the highest paid person in his profession.

Here you have someone who, in the eyes of the world, has everything, yet he walks out of his studio every day and says, "I'm not satisfied. This isn't enough. I'm still longing for more." Do you see the irony? A man who can't find satisfaction interviewed by a magazine named after a band famous for singing, "*I can't get no satisfaction...*".

Of course, this is not just a Howard Stern problem; it's is a human problem. The human heart is longing for satisfaction. Everybody is wanting to find fulfillment, and that's what Ecclesiastes is all about. It has been one of the main points made by Qoheleth throughout the book. He has come to that conclusion through a series of honest observations about life. Qoheleth, like Howard Stern, like the Rolling Stones, has concluded that true satisfaction is like chasing the wind. In Ecclesiastes 6, he says, ""*As I look at human beings going about living life, what I've discovered is the human heart is never satisfied.*" And also "*All the toil of man is for his mouth yet his appetite is not satisfied.*" Do you see what he was saying? He works to eat, yet he's always hungry. Now, that's food literally and metaphorically. They're all pursuing satisfaction, yet they can't get any.

He's not talking about enjoyment. This is an important distinction. When he's talking about desire and craving and wanting, he's not talking about it from the sense of enjoyment, he's talking about fulfillment. He's talking about having desires and wants and cravings for fulfillment. "If I could just get *that*, if I could just obtain *that*, then I'd have satisfaction, then I'd have fulfillment, then I would have meaning."

Let me bring it into our culture. It's Howard Stern, a $400 million contract, yet he says, "I'm still not satisfied." Michael Jordan, six titles, five MVPs, 10 scoring titles, 14 All-Star appearances, a billion-dollar shoe brand, and it is said of Michael, "He's constantly searching for release in golf or blackjack because the restlessness remains." Tom Brady, Super Bowl champ, Super Bowl MVP, Pro Bowl appearances, supermodel wife, says of all that, "There's got to be more than this." Shia LaBeouf, famous movie star, says, "I'm famous, yet I have no idea where this insecurity comes from." Madonna said, "I still have to prove that I am somebody. My struggle has never ended, and it probably never will."

Qoheleth has come to the same conclusion. He had everything you could ever want, and everything you could ever want isn't enough. Here are his reasons why.

Chapter Thirty-Four

"Avoid Your Birth"

E verything in life has a tendency to lose its luster. All of us have experienced that, whether it's in big ways or small ways. That thing we thought would satisfy didn't. There are reasons for that.

The first is a *desire reason*. *"All the toil of man is for his mouth, yet his appetite is not satisfied." (6:7)* Appetites by nature are ongoing. For example, you eat breakfast, and you're not shocked that you're hungry again for lunch. Nobody thinks, "Oh, I didn't think I would eat again. Where is this hunger coming from?" Nobody is shocked by that because we understand that the nature of appetite is that it is ongoing.

That's not just true with food. That's true with seasons of life. I took the themes in Ecclesiastes, and I put together a very generic kind of broad stroke of life. There were times in your life when what you desired most was pleasure. You wanted to hang out with friends. You wanted to have fun. Then there was a time when you focused on education, and some of you wanted to do well in school. Then there was a time when you focused on love and you wanted to find somebody you could marry.

Then, there was a time where you focused heavily on work or success. Then there was a time where you were focused on wealth and having things and possessions, and somewhere along the way, there was spirituality and pursuing spiritual things. Whether or not they were in that specific order for you, my point is your desires now are very different than your desires earlier in your life. At age 50, you will want things you didn't want at age 25. The seasons of life and desire change.

That's the nature of *appetite*.

Second, there's a *death reason*. *"Even though he should live a thousand years twice over, yet enjoy no good—do not all go to the one place?"* *(6:6)* The "one place" is death. "Do not all die?" Death makes everything in this life temporary, and temporary things can't satisfy the longings of our hearts. That's why it's vanity. Not that it's not enjoyable, not that it's not good; it just can't give you meaning.

Third, there is a *divine reason*. *"...a man to whom God gives wealth, possessions, and honor, so that he lacks nothing of all that he desires, yet God does not give him power to enjoy them, but a stranger enjoys them. This is vanity..."* *(6:2)* In other words, you have the delicious meal, but the cancer treatments took your taste buds away and you can't enjoy it. Qoheleth was saying what most of us at some point have probably wanted to say, namely, that it appears as if God is messing with you, and that he won't let you be fulfilled with the things you desire.

So, what should we do? Well, here's his advice to you: "Do the very best you can not to be born. Avoid your birth if at all possible." I'm not making it up. *"If a man fathers a hundred children and lives many years, so that the days of his years are many, but his soul is not satisfied with life's good things, and he also has no burial, I say that a stillborn child is better off than he."* (6:3)

Since avoiding your birth is not very practical, Qoheleth offers additional advice. *"Better is the sight of the eyes [what you see, what you have] than the wandering of the appetite: this also is vanity…" (6:9)* It's better to just enjoy what you have while you can than to spend all your life on this vain pursuit of desire to get everything you've ever wanted, which you may never get, and if you do it won't satisfy.

Chapter Thirty-Five

"The Problem is the Desire"

Qoheleth was right to say, "Be careful of your desires, of your cravings, of your wants, because they can lead you to a very dangerous place." Let me share three reasons he's right in that.

1. Desire can destroy relationships.

James 4:1 says, *"What causes quarrels and what causes fights among you?* [Why are you in conflict?] *Is it not this, that your passions are at war within you? You desire and do not have, so you murder. You covet and cannot obtain, so you fight and quarrel."*

The reason your marriage is so often in conflict, the reason your church is so often in conflict, the reason your coworkers are so often in conflict is because of what people want, because of desire. I have never walked by the bedroom of my children and heard them fighting about philosophical ideas. What I *have* heard is "I want that!" "You have what I desire."

Some of you reading this may have relationships that are a mess. It may be your marriage, a friendship, your relationship with a coworker, or a church member. What James is saying is that at the core, more often than not, somebody is threatening you want. Somebody is threatening your desire, and that's why your relationship is in shambles.

But it's not the only reason why.

2. Desire can create disillusionment.

When desires take over our lives, when wants and cravings consume us, it creates a warped sense of reality. You begin to view life in a way that isn't real.

There is a fable about a dog with carrying a bone. He's looking down into some water, and he sees what he thinks is *another* bone. He thinks, "Awesome! I can have two. Forget what I already have. Forget what is in my sight. I want more." He opens his mouth to get the other bone and drops the other one into the water and loses it.

Often our desires create an image, an illusion, and we buy into it thinking it's real and it will satisfy. Probably one of the best examples, would be pornography. It creates a fantasy world, a fantasy of desire, an illusion of a lie. The point is it begins to shape in our minds this view of reality that isn't real, and before we know it, we have no idea where we are.

3. Desire can lead to bad decisions.

Let me give you an example of this in Scripture. In Genesis chapter 25 we find the story of Jacob and Esau. Esau is the older brother. He has the inheritance which is everything in the ancient near East—the birthright. Look at what happens in Genesis 25:29:

> *Once when Jacob was cooking stew, Esau came in from the field, and he was exhausted. And Esau said to Jacob, 'Let me eat some of that red stew, for I am exhausted!' Jacob said, 'Sell me your birthright now.' Esau said, 'I am about to die; of what use is a birthright to me?' Jacob said, 'Swear to me now.' So he swore to him and sold his birthright to Jacob. Then Jacob gave Esau bread and lentil stew, and he ate and drank and rose and went his way. Thus Esau despised his birthright.*

An ancient near Eastern Jew would say, "That's insane! I don't care how hungry you are. You don't give up your inheritance. You don't give up your birthright for stew."

That's exactly what Ecclesiastes chapter 6 is saying. When life is controlled by your desires, you give up things you never thought you would. You never thought you'd be there. You never thought you'd go there. You never thought you'd do that. You never thought you'd compromise in that way. Why are you there? You're there because you didn't say no to the wanting and the craving and the desire, and it took you down the path of regret. You end up like the song June Carter wrote that Johnny Cash made famous: *"Bound by wild desire, I fell into a ring of fire."* What is that craving? What is that thing you're so hungry for you'd give up anything to have a bite?

It sounds awfully familiar to the Garden of Eden. "Just a bite. I promise it'll just be one bite." Before you know it, you look back and say, "Where am I?" You are where your desires have taken you.

You see, there's a sense in which Qoheleth is right when he says, *"Better is what you have than the wandering of the appetite."* Desire for fulfillment can lead to a dangerous place, but here's where he's wrong. The answer is not "Then say no to desire." Have you ever been around those Christians who are like, "Don't have fun with anything...No pleasure is allowed if you're going to follow Jesus?"

The question is... *What if our inability to be satisfied permanently with our desires was a sign of something else?* What if that was a pointer to something?

In the gospels, a large crowd is following Jesus. They're hungry. They find a little boy who has five loaves of bread and two fish. Jesus takes that, and he not only feeds the 5,000-plus; he feeds them the best meal they've had in a long time. The Bible says they ate their fill.

They're searching for Jesus the next day. Notice what is said in John 6:25. *"When they found him on the other side of the sea, they said to him, 'Rabbi, when did you come here?' Jesus answered them, 'Truly, truly,*

I say to you, you are seeking me, not because you saw signs [I'm the Messiah], but because you ate your fill of the loaves.'"

What's the issue in Ecclesiastes 6? A man toils for his mouth, but he's not satisfied. In other words, you work for food, but you're still hungry. What's happening in John 6? They ate their fill the day before, and they're hungry again the next day. Jesus says, "That's why you're coming back. You want more food."

Notice what Jesus says. *"Do not work for the food that perishes, but for the food that endures to eternal life which the Son of Man will give to you. For on him God the Father has set his seal."* (John 6:27) Jesus doesn't say, "What are you doing? You shouldn't desire. Don't you know Ecclesiastes says to limit that? Your appetites are a bad thing."

No. Jesus doesn't say the problem is the desire. Rather, the problem is the *focus* of the desire. It's not that you want; it's *what* you want. It's what you're craving. In other words, Qoheleth, when you say there can't be any satisfaction in this world, you're assuming the only bread there is, is in this world. What if there was a different source of food?

What if there was a different meal you could eat?

That's what makes John 6:35 so profound. *"Jesus said to them, 'I am the bread of life; whoever comes to me shall not hunger, and whoever believes in me shall never thirst.'"* You're right, Qoheleth, there is no satisfaction in food that is under the sun, but what if there's bread that came down out of heaven? What if there's food that's not of this world that if you desired it over anything else in this world you would never hunger again and never say, "I'm thirsty"? What *is* that food? It's a person, and his name is Jesus Christ. He's the Bread of Life.

C.S. Lewis said it best. *"The Christian says, 'Creatures are not born with desires unless satisfaction for those desires exists. A baby feels hunger: well, there is such a thing as food. A duckling wants to swim: well, [water exists to do it]. If I find in myself a desire which no experience in this world can satisfy, the most probable explanation is that I was made for another world."*

If I find in myself a craving nothing in this life can fulfill, it must mean I was created for another world. Qoheleth is right. God doesn't want you to find satisfaction in this life, because you weren't created for this life. You were created for him. God is not trying to frustrate you; He is trying to show you He loves you, because He wants to turn your cravings, turn your wants, turn your desires where they actually can be fulfilled.

The gospel answer is not "Avoid your birth and limit your desires." The gospel answer to the search of satisfaction is "Be born again and delight yourself in God."

Chapter Thirty-Six

"Banana Slices and the
Randomness of Life"

Every morning, he cuts his banana in exactly seven slices. Not six. Not eight. It has to be seven or something bad might happen to him that day. That is the morning routine of the famous film director Woody Allen, as described in an interview with *Newsweek* magazine. Allen said, "I know it would be total coincidence if I didn't slice [the banana] into seven pieces and my family were killed in a fire [that day]…but, you know, the guilt would be too much for me to bear, so it's easier for me to cut the stupid banana."

Most of us would find that behavior strange, but here's what's even stranger: Woody Allen is an atheist. Meaning, he believes this life is all there is. In fact, he even describes life as a "meaningless little flicker." Life is completely random.

This begs the question: "If life is random, Woody Allen, then why does it matter how you cut your banana?" It's why in the interview he admitted it's hard for him to reconcile his superstitions about life and his worldview on life. His answer is simply to say, "It's just been this way ever since I was five-years-old when I first realized death, when I first came into contact with death. Ever since then, I've not been able to shake the void."

When asked, "So why do you keep living?" Allen replied: "You know, I've never been able to come up with a good argument to choose life over death except I'm too scared. I'd rather just keep making movies, because it's easier to focus on how the hero will get out of his predicament than how I will get out of mine."

You have to stop for a minute and think about that. He's saying, "I believe that life is meaningless. I believe it's purely random, yet I'm obsessed with death. I can't get it off my mind. I slice my banana in exactly seven slices because I don't want anything bad to happen to me. All the while, I try to ignore that reality and fill the void by devoting myself to things in this life."

Sound familiar?

Woody Allen *is* Qoheleth, the difference being that Qoheleth isn't taking the perspective of an atheist. He believes in God. He just thinks God set it up this way. He knows God is sovereign but he believes that life appears random, and there's nothing worse that could happen to life than death.

So, what do you do? You fill your life in the void with as many things as you can to try to take your mind off it. Qoheleth does. Sex, pleasure, knowledge, work, success, love, money, power...on and on and on. Yet every time he arrives at the same conclusion, "Vanity, vanity, vanity."

He's really frustrated, and at the end of the book, he doesn't mind telling you how frustrated he is. *"Give a portion to seven, or even to eight, for you know not what disaster may happen on earth."* Look at verse five: *"As you do not know the way the spirit comes to the bones in the womb of a woman with child, so you do not know the work of God who makes everything. In the morning sow your seed, and at evening withhold not your hand, for you do not know which will prosper, this or that, or whether both alike will be good."* (11:5)

He's talking about life being frustrating because it's uncertain, because you can't predict it. Will you prosper? You don't know. Will disaster strike? You don't know. Will you be able to know what God is doing? You don't know. The most frustrating thing in life is not being able to figure out why.

It's like the roll of the dice. You're just hoping for a good bounce. You're hoping for a good hand. This is the way whether, you're rich or poor, healthy or not. It doesn't matter. This is life. There are no guarantees. It is a life full of uncertainty. Some of you will remember the song by Doris Day. The lyrics go like this...

> *When I was just a little girl,*
> *I asked my mother, "What will I be?*
> *Will I be pretty? Will I be rich?"*
> *Here's what she said to me.*

Que sera, sera,
Whatever will be, will be,
The future's not ours to see.

When I was young, I fell in love,
And I asked my sweetheart what lies ahead.
"Will we have rainbows, day after day?"
Here's what my sweetheart said.
Que sera, sera,
Whatever will be, will be,
The future's not ours to see.

Qoheleth would say, "That's insane! Whatever will be, will be? That's nuts! How in the world are you going to find meaning in life if whatever will be, will be?" Life is like those big heart boxes you get for Valentine's Day. You don't know if you're going to get the one that's filled with caramel or the one that's filled with toothpaste.

Forrest Gump's mother was right. Life is like a box of chocolates, because you never know what you're going to get. Although Qoheleth wouldn't put it that way. He's not writing *Hallmark* cards. He's not concerned with sentimentalism. He would say it *this* way.

"I saw that under the sun the race is not to the swift, nor the battle
to the strong, nor bread to the wise, nor riches to the intelligent,
nor favor to those with knowledge, but time and chance happen
to them all. For man does not know his time. Like fish that are
taken in an evil net, and like birds that are caught in a snare, so

the children of man are snared at an evil time, when it suddenly falls upon them." (9:11)

Here's your precious little *Hallmark* card. Are you ready? Life is not like a box of chocolates. Life is like a fish. You're swimming along. Everything is fantastic. Then all of a sudden, you're caught in a net, on somebody's dock, gasping for air, until eventually you get mounted on the wall.

How's that for a greeting card?

Life is frustrating. It's maddening, because you're just swimming along, and *Boom!* Net. It doesn't matter who you are. It doesn't matter where you're at in life. It doesn't matter if you're old or young. This life has one guarantee: *there aren't any.* Whatever will be, will be. When you add that to this next reality, it becomes even more maddening.

Chapter Thirty-Seven

"The Same Event
Happens to All"

"But all this I laid to heart, examining it all, how the righteous and the wise and their deeds are in the hand of God. Whether it is love or hate, man does not know; both are before him. It is the same for all, since the same event happens to the righteous and the wicked, to the good and the evil, to the clean and the unclean, to him who sacrifices and him who does not sacrifice. As the good one is, so is the sinner, and he who swears is as he who shuns an oath. This is an evil in all that is done under the sun, that the same event happens to all." (9:1)

dd a life full of uncertainty to a life that only has the certainty of death, and you will drive yourself crazy. As much as you might want to stick your head in the sand and act like this isn't the case, Qoheleth would say, "Open up your eyes and look around you."

In Ecclesiastes chapter 12, verse 3, he tells you what it's like to get old. *"...in the day when the keepers of the house tremble..."* Your hands begin to shake. *"...and the strong men are bent..."* Your legs become tired and weak. *"...and the grinders cease because they are few..."* *"...and those who look through the windows are dimmed..."*. You begin to lose your sight. *"...the doors on the street are shut—when the sound of the grinding is low..."*. You can't hear anymore. *"...they are afraid also of what is high, and terrors are in the way..."* You start getting nervous about things.

Keep reading—*"...the almond tree blossoms..."*. Have you ever seen almond trees blossom? They turn gray. They turn white. That's what your hair is going to look like. Unless, of course, it falls out. You used to have all this energy,"*...the grasshopper drags itself along,"* but now you'll find yourself napping anywhere.

Then it says: *"...and desire fails..."*. I think you know what that means. Now he has gotten to the point of death, *"...because man is going to his eternal home..."*. You see all this decay, old age, until finally there's death. After that, *"...the mourners go about the streets..."*—they have the funeral.

Verse six says, *"...before the silver cord is snapped, or the golden bowl is broken..."* In the ancient near East, that's the imagery of a light. In other words, Qoheleth is saying the light is gone, *"...or the pitcher is shattered at the fountain, or the wheel broken at the cistern..."*. In the ancient near East, it's very dry. Water is everything for any civilization, but particularly in the ancient near East, if you can't draw from the well, you have no source of life. Verse 7: *"...the dust returns to the earth as it was..."* That's a reversal of Genesis. You have dust and then spirit, and then what happens? You return to dust and your spirit goes to be with the Lord. *"...the spirit returns to God who gave it."* "

"Vanity of vanities, says the Preacher; all is vanity."

Here's his point—life is a candle, and it will soon be blown out. Qoheleth is saying, "As much uncertainty as there is in life, there is one certainty in life, and it's death."

Harry Houdini was the great escape artist who could get out of anything. He died on Halloween in 1929. He told his wife right before he died, "If there's a way out of death, I will make contact with you on the anniversary of my death." Ten years later, his wife, who had put a light underneath his picture, finally turned it out. The greatest escape artist who ever lived couldn't escape death.

Neither can we.

Qoheleth says you have to think about that. How do you make sense out of life when there are all of these uncertainties in life and the only certainty in life is death? You may think, "Well, okay, Qoheleth. Then how would you advise us to live? " Well, he always has advice for you. Here's what he would say are the three things you should do given that life is uncertain and death *is* certain.

1. Get busy living.

"Cast your bread upon the waters, for you will find it after many days." (11:1) That's a very difficult verse to translate. Most scholars believe it's the idea of sea trading. Casting bread on the water was very risky

215   FELTNER

for them to go out to sea and to gather goods and come back, but if they survived the journey, there was great reward. So, the verse is talking about risk-taking, stepping out there, casting your bread on the water, taking risk, and not being afraid.

Now, that makes sense when you compare it to chapter 11, verse 4: *"He who observes the wind will not sow, and he who regards the clouds will not reap."* So, what's he contrasting there? He's describing a farmer who's watching the clouds, waiting for the perfect weather conditions before he sows the seed. Do any of you know somebody who is so analytical they end up doing nothing? They analyze everything.

It takes an hour to decide where you're going to go eat because you're thinking about every single possible scenario. Qoheleth is saying: "If life is uncertain and death is certain, then why would you just sit there paralyzed doing nothing? Get busy living! Take risk. Step out there. Cast your bread on the water."

In the movie *The Bucket List*, with Jack Nicholson and Morgan Freeman, there's a scene where they're going through their lists, and they're talking about those things they want to do before they die. They just found out they only have one year left to live, so they're thinking about how to strategize that final year. Here's what Jack Nicholson's character says to Morgan Freeman: "You think 45 years went by fast? Imagine one. So, we can either lie around hoping for a miracle through some science experiment or we can put some moves on."

Your life is a candle that will soon be blown out. So, get busy moving!

2. Get busy giving.

"Give a portion to seven, or even to eight..." Why? *"...for you know not what disaster may happen on earth." (11:2)* Understanding that verse should be rather simple. *"Give seven, or even eight, because you don't know what's going to happen."*

"I'll be generous when the kids are gone. I'll be generous in December when I need to make up for some tax deductions. I'll be generous when I retire." You don't know if that'll ever happen. You don't even know if you'll be here at the end of the year. You don't even know if you'll make retirement.

Why would you hold back on being generous? Why would you hold back on giving when you have the opportunity to be generous now? If you understand that life is uncertain and death *is*, then it's insane to think, "I'm just going to hold on to everything." Give, be generous, because life is a candle that will soon be blown out.

3. Get busy enjoying.

"Light is sweet, and it is pleasant for the eyes to see the sun. So if a person lives many years, let him rejoice in them all..." (11:7)
"Rejoice, O young man, in your youth, and let your heart cheer you in the days of your youth. Walk in the ways of your heart and the sight of your eyes." (11:9)

In other words, stop and smell the roses. Enjoy the delicious steak. Cherish that moment with that sweet baby on your lap. Enjoy the sound of the crack of a bat as it hits the ball, the beautiful sunset at the cabin. Enjoy what you can while you can, because your life is a candle that will soon be blown out.

That sounds like good advice, doesn't it? I mean, given that life is uncertain and death *is* certain, then it makes sense that the best you could do in the middle, is get busy living, get busy giving, and get busy enjoying. You need to know why Qoheleth is giving you this advice.

This is really important for the Woody Allen's of the world.

Chapter Thirty-Eight

"Hope in the Face of Death"

"So if a person lives many years, let him rejoice in them all; but let him remember that the days of darkness will be many. All that comes is vanity. Rejoice, O young man. But know that for all these things God will bring you into judgment." — Ecclesiastes 11:8-9

"Remember also your Creator in the days of your youth, before the evil days come and the years draw near of which you will say, 'I have no pleasure in them...'" — Ecclesiastes 12:1

As we have just seen, life is uncertain, death *is* certain, so live, give, and enjoy. Why? It's the only thing that can take your mind off of what's coming. You've known death is lingering since you were five-years-old, Woody Allen, so the best you can do is devote yourself to making movies, hoping you can forget, if just for a little while, that death is coming for you. It's a temporary distraction from life's ultimate predicament.

This is not just for Woody Allen. It's also for you and me. "How do WE make sense out of the uncertainty of life given the certainty of death?

In the beginning, God created man and woman. He created humanity, and he gave them abundance. They were able to live and give and enjoy in freedom. God told them, "Don't eat of this particular tree," and they disobeyed. They rebelled, and the Bible says the wages of sin is death. Because of sin, creation is fallen. It was subjected to a curse, and yes, that's why it's messed up. That's why, by its appearance, it doesn't make any sense at all. That's why our bodies will decay. That's why we will all face death. Qoheleth is right, except for this: just because *you* can't get out of the predicament of death doesn't mean there's not a way out of death. What if there's a hero who got out of the predicament?"

That, dear friends, is the good news of the gospel of Jesus Christ. The Bible says that Jesus became a man. He came into the world. He took on flesh. He took on a body, amazingly, that's like ours. It would bleed, and it would be beaten, and it was crucified on the cross.

Look at Hebrews 2:14-15, *"Since therefore the children share in flesh and blood, he himself likewise partook of the same things [he became a man], that through death he might destroy the one who has the power of death, that is, the devil, and deliver all those who through fear of death were subject to lifelong slavery.*" Jesus became a man like us, and he died our death.

That's great news, but it keeps getting better. Not only did Jesus die, but he defeated death by walking out of the grave. Listen to 2 Timothy 1:10: *"...and which now has been manifested through the appearing of our Savior Christ Jesus, who abolished death and brought life and immortality to light through the gospel..."* So, Jesus came and died our death, but he defeated death and is victorious over the grave.

It gets even better than that. Because he conquered, *you* can conquer. It means because you can't get out of your predicament, but Jesus got out of the predicament, you can get out of it in him. Jesus said in John 11:25, *"I am the resurrection and the life. Whoever believes in me, though he die, yet shall he live, and everyone who lives and believes in me shall never die."*

As the Apostle Paul writes in Romans 8: *"No, in all these things we are more than conquerors through him who loved us. For I am sure that neither death nor life, nor angels nor rulers, nor things present nor things to come, nor powers, nor height nor depth, nor anything [under the sun], will be able to separate us from the love of God in Christ Jesus our Lord."*

Qoheleth says, "Life is uncertain. Death is certain. You'd better fill your void with the things of this life." The gospel says, "Life is uncertain. Death is certain, so you'd better fill your life with the promise of eternal life, which is in the champion, the conqueror, the defeater of death and the giver of life, Christ Jesus. Then you can get busy living, and you can get busy giving, and you can get busy enjoying. Why? Because you're not afraid anymore."

Qoheleth is saying, "You live, give, and enjoy because it takes your mind off death." The gospel says, "Live, give, and enjoy because Jesus defeated death and you don't have to live in fear."

Billy Graham, when he was brought to the capitol to receive the Congressional Medal of Honor, was in a room filled with pictures and statues of famous Americans throughout American history. Dr. Graham stood up. I want you to picture this. There's the vice president. There are the senators and congressmen and evangelical leaders all filling the room. A special moment. He looks at all of them, and points to the pictures on the wall of all of those famous people in American history. He says, "What do every single one of them have in common?" There's this awkward silence, and he says, "They're all dead."

He proceeded to tell everyone in the room how they could have eternal life in Christ Jesus.

Life is uncertain and death is certain, and your only way out is Jesus Christ. You're not going to find meaning by ignoring death. You're only going to find meaning in the one who died and rose again. In a world that is full of uncertainties, where people anxiously slice their bananas and make their bucket lists, it is only by faith in Jesus Christ that you will ever rest in peace.

Chapter Thirty-Nine

"A Story Within a Story"

I t's one of the most classic love stories ever told. There's a beautiful princess kidnapped by an evil prince and forced to marry him. All the while, the man she loves is trying to save her. There's death. There's danger. There's a struggle for power and the search for love. I'm referring to that classic 1987 movie, *The Princess Bride*. If you know the story, you know it's actually more than just a fairy tale about love. There's actually a story behind the story.

It's actually about a grandfather and his grandson. The grandson is sick. He's staying home from school and the grandfather comes over with a book, and they to read it together. As the story develops, as things begin to progress, you find that so does their relationship. When the movie is over, you discover the story isn't just about love, or a struggle for power; it's about a grandfather who's teaching his grandson about life.

That is how you need to view the book of Ecclesiastes. Qoheleth is a wise and honest man. He is someone, the Bible tells us, who had more knowledge than anybody in Jerusalem before him. He cheered his body with wine. He gave himself to every pleasure. He built houses and vineyards. He had the treasure of kings, and he turned over every rock under the sun trying to find meaning in life. He still couldn't find what he was looking for.

Now we come to the final chapter of the book. The curtain pulls back, and you see the story behind the story. You see what has been going on the entire time has not just been all of the details of Qoheleth and his search for meaning. You see something else has been taking place. *"Besides being wise, the Preacher [Qoheleth] also taught the people knowledge..."* (12:9)

Did you notice how the voice changed? Did you notice how, all of a sudden, it's in third person? If you remember, that's how the book starts. *"The words of the Preacher..."* You see the same voice. *"...the son of David, king in Jerusalem. Vanity of vanities, says the Preacher..."* (1:1)

It has now shifted back to the narrator of the book. So, what's the identity of the narrator? Who is this voice who's speaking at the end? Well, we don't know his name. We don't know his identity, but we do have an idea as to his relationship. *"My son, beware of anything beyond these."* (12:12)

If you know much about Wisdom Literature in the Old Testament, you know this is a lot like Proverbs. It's a genre where a father is teaching his son about wisdom and life. The story behind the story. There's actually a father who's using this story of Qoheleth, like in *The Princess Bride*, to teach his son about life. So, what are those lessons his son needs to learn? What are those lessons you and I need to learn as a result of this book?

> "*Besides being wise, [Qoheleth] also taught the people knowledge, weighing and studying and arranging many proverbs with great care. The Preacher sought to find words of delight, and uprightly he wrote words of truth. The words of the wise are like goads, and like nails firmly fixed are the collected sayings; they are given by one Shepherd. My son, beware of anything beyond these. Of making many books there is no end, and much study is a weariness of the flesh.*" (12:9)

The narrator, or father, now gives his evaluation of Qoheleth's observations. First, he says Qoheleth has taught knowledge and arranged proverbs with care. He's accurate. He's precise in what he said. Second, he wrote words of truth. What Qoheleth said is right. What he said is honest. You may not like what you heard, but that doesn't make what you heard less true. These were words of truth and wisdom. To the point that the father can say, "*Beware of anything beyond these.*" Everything that needed to be said has been said. "Son, he is wise, and you need to listen to him."

There are three things the father is teaching his son through Qoheleth, and three things this book of Ecclesiastes is teaching us.

---

1. Life under the sun is a struggle.

"Then I said in my heart, 'What happens to the fool will happen to me also. Why then have I been so very wise?' And I said in my heart that this also is vanity. For of the wise as of the fool there is no enduring remembrance, seeing that in the days to come all will have been long forgotten. How the wise dies just like the fool! So I hated life, because what is done under the sun was grievous to me, for all is vanity and a striving after wind. I hated all my toil in which I toil under the sun, seeing that I must leave it to the man who will come after me, and who knows whether he will be wise...?" (2:15)

Qoheleth has struggled throughout his journey. He has said some hard things. This is why most preachers don't preach on this book, and it's why a lot of Christians don't like the book. Qoheleth is inviting you into the struggle. You see, most people try to gloss over the reality of life. The reality is, life is fallen. Life, while beautiful, is broken.

Christians of all people ought to know this. We ought to understand more than anybody else that this is how life is, because we have the Bible. The Apostle Paul said, in Romans 8:18: *"For I consider that the sufferings of this present time are not worth comparing with the glory that is to be revealed to us."* In other words, life is not sugar and spice and everything nice. Real life is not pretty kittens and ribbons. Real life is a struggle.

2. Life under the sun has no solutions.

"What is crooked cannot be made straight, and what is lacking cannot be counted." (1:15) This is clearly Qoheleth's main proverb, one that summarizes everything. Life is a question you can't answer. It's a problem you can't solve. Throughout this whole search, he has been trying to answer the question of "What gives life meaning? How do you make sense out of this?" He has tried everything. But nothing under the sun answers life's ultimate questions.

They can't solve that problem.

It doesn't matter how many Harvard degrees you have. All that education won't give you the answer about why your spouse died at 30. There's not enough knowledge in the world to answer that question. There's not enough alcohol in the world to answer that question. There's not enough résumé-building to answer that question.

"My son, beware of anything beyond these. Of making many books there is no end, and much study is a weariness of the flesh." (12:12) What he's saying is, "Think about all of the books we have." Think of all of the books that have been written. Think about all of the books that line the shelves of your office, of libraries, at schools, yet we still are searching for answers. We have a whole lot of books but not a lot of answers.

3. Life under the sun can't bring satisfaction.

Look back at chapter six: *"There is an evil that I have seen under the sun, and it lies heavy on mankind: a man to whom God gives wealth, possessions, and honor, so that he lacks nothing of all that he desires..."* He gets everything his heart desired. ...yet God does not give him power to enjoy them, but a stranger enjoys them. This is vanity; it is a grievous evil.

If you pursue knowledge, you end up with more questions. If you pursue pleasure, it keeps you coming back for more. If you pursue success, you're either always trying to get to the top or you're always trying to stay at the top. If it's love, well, soul mates die. If it's money, it will likely be left to a squanderer. If it's power, you're likely to abuse it, and all the while death lingers, making everything in life short-term.

The father is telling the son, "Pay careful attention to this. Life under the sun is a struggle, life under the sun cannot ultimately give you solutions, and life under the sun will not bring you ultimate satisfaction. So, I want to teach you, son, how you live. Given that what Qoheleth has said is right, I want to teach you how to live in light of that truth."

Look now at verse 13 in chapter 12. *"The end of the matter..."* Here's the conclusion. *"...all has been heard."* We've heard everything Qoheleth has had to say, and he has been right. *"Fear God and keep his commandments, for this is the whole duty of man. For God will bring every deed into judgment, with every secret thing, whether good or evil."* In other words, Qoheleth was right as far as he went, but he didn't give you the best solution. He didn't give you the right solution. The doctor was right on diagnosis but wrong on cure. This is the only way you will find meaning in life...

Chapter Forty

"The Secret to a Meaningful Life"

F amous evangelical pastor Tony Evans describes the fear of God this way: "The old belief, centuries ago, was that the sun revolved around the earth. As we now know, this belief was wrong. The earth revolves around the sun. Many of us have got it wrong in our spiritual lives. God doesn't revolve around us. We revolve around him. We know that we fear God when we have made him the centerpiece of our lives."

Do you see how that's different from Qoheleth? "The best you can do is live for you." The father is saying, "Oh, no, no, no, son. The best you can do is fear God. Make him the centerpiece of your life." Second, "keep his commands rather than obeying your desires."

This isn't just "Keep the rules." It's not about legalism. Don't read this as saying you just have to follow the rules. He's talking about this: you have to trust God, as the Creator of life, that he knows what's best *for* life. The way he structured it, the way he designed it, the way he created it, is the best way.

It's not how *you* want to live it. It's not the desires *you* want to have. It's, instead, the pattern God has put in life, and we are to pursue that. We want to live life the way God has called us to live life, not how we want to live it. It's why in the first Psalm, we see that beautiful imagery of a man who is meditating on God's law, day and night. He says it is his delight. Why is that? Because God's commandments are not restrictions *to* our pleasure; they are guidelines *for* our pleasure.

When you live according to the design God has given, it's all the more enjoyable. It's like a "road closed" sign on the highway. Sure, you may be frustrated that you have to go a different way, but most of us fully understand that the detour was put in place, as frustrating as it may be, for your safety, for your good, for your health. The same is that of the commands of God.

We fear God rather than live for self, we keep his commands rather than obey our desires, because of eternity. We don't believe this is all there is. We don't believe this life is all there will be, so we're living in light of the future. We're preparing ourselves for eternal life.

We're going to be tempted, just as the father knows his son will be tempted, to be shortsighted, to live for the now, to be narrow focused. So, the father is calling his son back. You have to understand that eternity is in perspective in how we live. We will stand before God.

We have to learn to live by faithful obedience, not because life makes sense but because it doesn't. Because life doesn't make sense is all the more reason you have to live a life of faith. Living by obedient faith when life doesn't make sense is the only way you can make sense out of life. That's what the father is teaching the son.

This is so beautiful how the end of Ecclesiastes gives us two very clear ways of living. You can live *this* way. You can focus on yourself, following your own desires, because you believe this is all you have *or* you can focus on God, follow his pattern and commands, because you're living with an eternal perspective. The whole point of Ecclesiastes is that it's only the latter that finds meaning. It's only the one who steps back and says, "This isn't about me anymore; I'm fully surrendered to God and his ways for the sake of eternity" who actually makes sense out of life.

Where would one start to find how this life can be lived? Pay close attention to the language the father uses... *"The words of the wise are like goads, and like nails firmly fixed are the collected sayings; they are given by one Shepherd." (12:11)*

Isn't that interesting?

Remember, this book is divinely inspired. The ultimate author is God. So, what's the point? He's saying that wisdom, the ability to understand life, is like firmly fixed nails that are given by one Shepherd. Why would the book end that way? Why would the divine author put that in as the book closes? Here's why: because you and I are Qoheleth, every one of us. We're just like him. We are looking to things and chasing after things to give us meaning.

Isaiah says it in Isaiah 53:6: *"All we like sheep have gone astray; we have turned—every one—to his own way and the Lord has laid on him the iniquity of us all."* We are all running this way and that way. We're running all over the place, yet what we don't realize is we're never going to find meaning without a shepherd.

Jesus said in John 10:7, *"Truly, truly, I say to you, I am the door of the sheep. [...] If anyone enters by me, he will be saved and will go in and out and find pasture [find meaning]. The thief comes only to steal and kill and destroy. I came that they may have life and have it abundantly. I am the good shepherd. The good shepherd lays down his life for the sheep."*

Don't you see? Jesus has been the answer to every search throughout the book of Ecclesiastes and for your life, as well. If it's knowledge you seek, Jesus is wisdom. If it's pleasure you seek, Jesus turns water into the best wine. If it's money you want, Jesus gives a kingdom currency that will not be destroyed. If you hunger, Jesus is the Bread of Life. If it's love you desire, yet your loved one dies, Jesus offers a love that not even death can separate you from.

Do you feel like life is just a treadmill? Jesus came into the treadmill and broke the pattern so you could have life abundantly. If it's death you're concerned about, take heart. This Good Shepherd laid his life down for the sheep and conquered the grave. The answer to your search is the Shepherd, Jesus Christ.

So, whatever your search is (and it's something), you need a shepherd. You need Jesus Christ to guide you, if you want to make sense out of life.

As Saint Augustine said, our hearts are restless until they find Him.